ROUTLEDGE LIBRARY EDITIONS:
TRADE UNIONS

I0127692

Volume 21

TRADE UNIONS
AND THE LAW

TRADE UNIONS
AND THE LAW

HORATIO VESTER
and
ANTHONY H. GARDNER

Routledge
Taylor & Francis Group

LONDON AND NEW YORK

First published in 1955 by Methuen & Co. Ltd.

This edition first published in 2023
by Routledge
4 Park Square, Milton Park, Abingdon, Oxon OX14 4RN

and by Routledge
605 Third Avenue, New York, NY 10158

Routledge is an imprint of the Taylor & Francis Group, an informa business

British Library Cataloguing in Publication Data
A catalogue record for this book is available from the British Library

ISBN: 978-1-032-37553-3 (Set)
ISBN: 978-1-032-39586-9 (Volume 21) (hbk)
ISBN: 978-1-032-39594-4 (Volume 21) (pbk)
ISBN: 978-1-003-35044-6 (Volume 21) (ebk)

DOI: 10.4324/9781003350446

Publisher's Note
The publisher has gone to great lengths to ensure the quality of this reprint but points out that some imperfections in the original copies may be apparent.

Disclaimer
The publisher has made every effort to trace copyright holders and would welcome correspondence from those they have been unable to trace.

Trade Unions and the Law

*

HORATIO VESTER
Barrister-at-Law

and

ANTHONY H. GARDNER
O.B.E., T.D.

METHUEN & CO. LTD, LONDON
36 *Essex Street, Strand, WC2*

First published in 1955

CATALOGUE NO. 5763/U

PRINTED AND BOUND IN GREAT BRITAIN BY
RICHARD CLAY AND COMPANY, LTD., BUNGAY, SUFFOLK

CONTENTS

INTRODUCTION

IN this book we attempt to make the law of trade unions intelligible to the reader without legal training.

Our reason for embarking on so rash an undertaking is that to far too many people the law affecting trade unions is the *terra incognita* of the modern scene. Yet there is hardly a person who is not affected by their activities.

We have sought to outline our subject in a manner which is at once simple and clear enough to be understood by the general reader, and sufficiently precise, detailed, and accurate to be of assistance and guidance to the intelligent trade unionist or student, or any other person who may wish to know what constitutes a trade union or what his rights or duties are in relation to a trade union.

Those who wish to delve deeper should consult the works of the Rt. Hon. Sir Henry Slesser, P.C., and Mr N. A. Citrine, which we found of great assistance.

Under the present law, trade unions enjoy certain rights and immunities that have not been conferred on other associations. We refer to them collectively as privileges, because privileges is the word which, in its proper sense, most accurately conveys the effect of the law.

Unfortunately it is also a word that is often misused. It has acquired connotations that are both emotional and political.

In this book we use the word privilege in its strict legal sense only.

H. V.

A. H. G.

4 *Brick Court,*

Temple, E.C.4   *January,* 1955

CHAPTER I

THE TRADE UNION SYSTEM

ACCORDING to Kipling:

'There are nine and sixty ways of constructing tribal lays
And – every – single – one – of – them – is – right.'

There are probably as many possible definitions of a trade union—all correct from some point of view.

There is also a statutory definition—that is, one contained in an Act of Parliament.

Sydney and Beatrice Webb in their *History of Trade Unions*, say: 'A trade union, as we understand the term, is a continuous association of wage-earners for the purpose of maintaining the conditions of their working lives.' This is a description of the sort of trade union in which they were interested. But as a definition of trade unions generally it leaves something to be desired.

The subject of this book is what the law considers to be a trade union. It includes many types of association. Some are temporary associations. Some are associations that fall within the Webbs' definition. Some are not associations of wage-earners at all, such as federations of employers or organizations of professional people.

If we were asked to give a short general definition of what the law considers to be a trade union, we should say that it is a device to enable a group or class in trade or industry to bargain with any other group or class, and as such it is one of the master organizations of the present industrial system.

Trade unions exist because they are necessary. The industrial system of this country today would have difficulty in functioning without them. It is no doubt for this reason that Parliament has given them the privileged position that they enjoy under the law.

In bygone days a handloom-weaver working in his cottage might be reasonably independent. If he could not get his raw material, or find a market for his wares, he was at least a member of a small community with other resources and other possible sources of employment. But when he moved to a town of wool-weavers, with wool-weaving as its sole reason for existence, he became a minute unit in a large pool of labour. Standing alone and competing with all the other weavers, his position was far from happy.

Improved transport had brought the country closer together. In some cases this meant that a manufacturer could sell his goods in a much larger market. He could trade in all parts of the country, instead of being limited to his own district. So could his competitors, of many of whom he had never even heard.

When industry was scattered in small units it may not have been too difficult, as a general rule, for a man to get a fair price for his wares or a fair wage for his labour. Sometimes wages were fixed by custom.

There was, however, no custom affecting the steam-engine or the power-loom, and the people who controlled them had little respect for the out-moded customs of a previous age.

The section of the community which was the most unfavourably affected by these changes were workmen and wage-earners of one kind and another. Their numbers were greatly increased, and whatever economic security they had previously enjoyed vanished. Economists have pointed out that although labour is in one sense a commodity, like most other things, it has certain features that are very unfavourable to the vendor, that is, the labourer. It will not keep, and the vendor has to deliver it personally to the purchaser at the place where and the time when it is wanted.

In combining together into associations for their own protection, workmen saw a means of strengthening their bargaining powers *vis-à-vis* their employers, and of righting the economic scale that had tilted against them. Such associations had, of course, existed long before the Industrial Revolution, but the need for them became imperative, and they were given new vitality when industry became vast, impersonal, and specialized.

Employers and traders had for many centuries combined into associations for the protection of their trade interests. Now they combined into new federations to meet the challenge of the workers' associations. Parliament chose to call all these combinations trade unions.

It is perhaps unfortunate that the public at large hears much about the activities of trade unions in relation to strikes, lock-outs, and other industrial crises, or in relation to politics, but very little about their day-to-day work in hammering out the master agreements that govern modern industry, and in ironing out the countless petty grievances that would otherwise lead to trouble. The complexity of their work is very great. The terms and conditions on which a man works may well comprehend compulsory provisions required by law, provisions that are the result of arbitrations fought before industrial courts or arbitrators, and the provisions of national and regional agreements that have been negotiated between the two sides. All these have to be kept up to date and are subject to constant alteration and revision. The pay packet of every man in industry depends to some extent on this complex machinery.

WORDS

We find it necessary in this book to use a number of words in a legal sense, or possibly in an unusual sense. In order to assist readers who may not be familiar with the usage, we set out the words below with the meaning which we employ.

A 'statute' is a law contained in an Act of Parliament. In this country Parliament is supreme and it is the duty of the courts to enforce the laws enacted by Parliament, regardless of whether or not they conflict with the principles of common law or equity.

'Common law' is used in two senses. In its wider sense it means judge-made law, as opposed to statute law, that is to say, the principles of law contained in all the accumulated judgements of the courts.

In the narrow sense it means the law that was administered in the old Courts of Common Law as distinguished from the law administered in the old Court of Chancery, which was called 'equity'. Since the Judicature Act 1873 all Divisions of the High Court administer both common law and equity.

There is a further instrument used by law-makers today that requires a word, and that is the 'statutory order'. Parliament frequently passes an Act that deals only with the broad outlines of a subject, and gives some Minister power to fill in the details by means of orders. When such orders have been approved by Parliament they have the force of a statute. These orders play an increasing part in modern legislation.

Law can also be divided into 'civil law' and 'criminal law'. 'Civil law' is that which is concerned with the private rights and obligations arising between man and man. 'Criminal law' deals with matters which a man is ordered to do or abstain from doing for the public good and for the neglect of which he can be punished.

Important divisions of the civil law are the law of contract and the law of tort. A 'tort' is a civil wrong for which damages can be recovered, such as libel, nuisance, or negligence.

What the law understands by a 'contract' or 'agreement' is some bargain made between two or more persons in which there is some right or property or something of value at stake. Such an agreement the courts will enforce either directly, or by awarding damages against a party who breaks it. They will interpret it by a declaration for the assistance of the parties, and may restrain a party from breaking it by an injunction.

A 'trust' arises where property is held under a legal obligation to use it for specific purposes, or to hold it for the benefit of some other person. The person who holds the property is called the 'trustee'.

A 'bond' is a document under seal in which a man undertakes to pay a sum of money in a certain event. In days gone by it was a common form of legal instrument, and often took the form of a promise to pay a large sum if the man giving the bond, or someone else, defaulted in the payment of a smaller sum. Bonds are not now of common use.

'Friendly Societies' are voluntary associations formed for the purpose of forming a fund for the payment of benefits to members, their wives or children, in sickness, infancy, old age, or infirmity. They provide a very useful form of insurance. They can be registered or unregistered. They often bear a superficial resemblance to trade unions, as the form of organization (that is, the sub-division into branches and areas) is often the same.

Many trade unions have objects that are similar to those of a Friendly Society, but a Friendly Society is not a trade union.

An 'Industrial and Provident Society' is a society registered under the Industrial & Provident Societies Acts. The purpose of these societies (which gave them their name) is that they should be industrial, in the sense that members combine together to make profits out of some joint undertaking, and provident, in the sense that they divide the profits among the members, if possible, in such a way as to make provision for ill health, unemployment, or old age.

In their best-known form these societies are represented by the Co-operative Societies, where the members, through the society, engage in some trade and their profits are divided among the members in the form of a dividend, not on capital invested, but on the price of the goods and services dealt with by the member through the society.

These societies bear no resemblance whatever to trade unions, and are not subject to trade union law.

We use the expressions 'craft union' and 'general union'. These are popular expressions, and have no statutory meaning.

In a craft union some craft qualification is necessary. This generally takes the form of requiring that members serve a term of apprenticeship under regulations laid down or approved by the union. The workmen's unions in existence at the time the first of the modern Trade Union Acts became law in 1871 were craft unions. As a rule, they attached great importance to their benevolent objects, and provided their members with substantial benefits in the case of sickness or unemployment. They did not assist the vast body of unskilled working men: first, because they required a craft qualification, and secondly, because they called for substantial contributions from members in order to maintain the benefits of one kind and another that they provided for their members.

'General unions' are those which are open to all workers and have no craft qualification for membership. They are sometimes called industrial unions when they are organized on an industrial basis. They normally try to maintain the contributions of members at the lowest possible figure so as not to impose too great a burden on the wages of an unskilled labourer.

CHAPTER II

HISTORICAL INTRODUCTION

ATTEMPTS have been made to trace a connexion between the workmen's trade unions, as they exist today, and the medieval trade or craft guilds. It is difficult to show any close link between them. A more likely origin is the fraternity of journeymen which came into existence on the decay of the old guild system. These seem to have been the first true combinations of workmen in this country, banded together to try to get better pay and working conditions. In one form or another they have existed ever since.

From the fourteenth century onwards there have been attempts by Parliament to regulate wages and conditions of labour, and to prevent combinations of workmen in what we should now call trade unions. As time went on the system of regulating wages by statute fell into disuse, while the laws intended to stifle trade unions were more and more vigorously enforced.

This is perhaps not remarkable. All such laws had to be enforced by the local Justices of the Peace, who were frequently local employers. Almost all government officials and officers, entrusted with maintaining law and order, had a profound dislike and fear of anything that savoured of conspiracy or the secret society, and in their view the trade unions of the day savoured of both.

These trends reached their peak in 1800. The Combination Act passed in that year made it illegal for workmen to combine for the purpose of improving their wages or conditions of labour, or to organize or attend meetings for such

7

purposes. This oppressive piece of legislation sprang largely from the fear of the revolutionary ideas that were at that time radiating from France.

The Combination Act 1800 was repealed in 1824, and from that year until the passing of the first of the modern Trade Union Acts in 1871 there was comparatively little restrictive legislation directed at workmen's combinations. Some unions which had managed to maintain an underground existence were able to come out into the open, but they were still in a difficult and hazardous position because of the aspects of the common law with which we shall shortly deal.

The Industrial Revolution created a new impetus, by increasing labours' need for organization. The factory system, with the consequent concentration of industry in large centres, the increasing demand for semi-skilled or unskilled labour, the lack of alternative employment in bad times, the harsh economic doctrine of the time, with its insistence on the moral and material benefits of uncontrolled competition, the belief that a pool of unemployed labour upon which industry could draw was indispensable to a healthy economy —all these made it obvious that unless the working man could develop some effective machinery for collective bargaining with his employer he would have little hope of improving his economic condition or getting a fair share of the profits of industry.

With time the temper of the age changed. The ideas of the Benthamite reformers spread, and it also may have begun to appear at least to some of the manufacturers and traders that they themselves might wish to combine to regulate prices and the terms upon which they would sell their goods. Thus between 1800 and 1871 the universal fear and distrust of trade unions gradually gave way to a recognition that they and the trade-union movement had a part to play in the modern world.

To succeed in discharging its functions, a trade union required sufficient continuity of existence to enable it to represent its members in collective bargaining. It also needed means of forcing its members to accept restrictions on their individual freedom of action, so that the union could enforce its policy by withholding labour, if it were a workmen's union, or by withholding employment, goods, or services, if it were an employer's or trader's union.

This involved an invasion of the liberty of the individual which was contrary to principles of the common law and equity—principles which had been developed by judges over hundreds of years, which were intended to protect the freedom of the individual.

Thus after the Combination Acts had been repealed in 1824 trade unions still found their activities closely circumscribed by the law. Two aspects of the law in particular threatened to stifle them. On the civil side there was the doctrine of restraint of trade, which had the effect of vitiating their contracts and trusts, and on the criminal side there was the misdemeanour of conspiracy, which threatened their leaders and members with imprisonment.

The principle of law which makes activities in restraint of trade unlawful is based on what lawyers call public policy. In the eyes of the law, public policy demands that every man should be at liberty to work as hard as he can, and to sell the fruits of his labour and skill for the best price he can get. Therefore any bargain that he makes which unreasonably fetters him in the exercise of these rights is unlawful as tending to deprive the state of the benefits to be derived from the full exercise of his industry and skill.

It is a principle that can be expressed in general terms without difficulty; but when the principle comes to be applied to the facts of any particular case, difficulties arise. It is not every interference with or restraint of trade that is unlawful. It is only when the restraint becomes unreasonable,

B

or greater than is necessary for the protection of the parties, that it becomes unlawful. It is in each case a question of degree.

To give an example: if a man by hard work and aptitude creates a profitable business, he has the right to sell it with its goodwill, and thus reap the reward of his labour. To the purchaser the value of the business may largely depend on the vendor agreeing not to compete with him after the sale. Such an agreement may offend against the rule unless it is strictly limited to what is reasonable and necessary to protect the purchaser. If the contract goes beyond this, by creating greater restraints than are reasonable and necessary, it is illegal—or, at least that part of it which imposes the unreasonable restraint.

It is not illegal by statute. It is illegal because it offends against one of the principles of common law.

It is illegal not in the sense that it is a crime, but only in the sense that the courts will do nothing to enforce it. This principle may be far-reaching when applied to the rules of an association. It results in the association being unable to enforce its contracts, administer its trusts, or protect its property.

Of course it is not impossible to form an association for collective bargaining which does not offend against this rule, but in any case in which the executive of the association was given power to withhold the labour of its members (that is, to call a strike), the courts had no hesitation in holding that the association was unlawful in the sense we have indicated.

The second principle of common law that threatened the existence of the unions between 1825 and 1871 was that which underlies the indictable misdemeanour of conspiracy. It has been defined as 'the agreement of two or more to do an unlawful act, or to do a lawful act by unlawful means'. Thus if either the object of the combination or the means to be used in carrying it out were unlawful, an offence was committed. It is difficult to imagine a full-blooded trade dispute involving strike action which does not in some way contravene this principle, and as a result trade-union leaders carried on their work in the shadow of the threat of prosecution.

It was against this background that the Royal Commission to inquire into trade unions was appointed in 1867. As a result of its deliberations the Trade Union Act 1871 became law.

It is the first of a series of statutes intended as a shelter under which trade unions can operate. The Trade Union Acts metaphorically create a protective umbrella under which conspiracy can no longer be prosecuted and contrácts in restraint of trade are no longer illegal, and where there is a privileged position for those who are permitted to shelter.

The objects of the first of these Acts—the Trade Union Act 1871—were limited. They were:

1. To modify the law of criminal conspiracy.
2. To extend the protection of the law to the property, contracts, and trusts of trade unions.
3. To encourage unions to become respectable by voluntarily bringing themselves under the wing of the law by registering as trade unions.

The Act in fact had unexpected consequences. In some ways it achieved its object, in others it failed, and in still others its effect was more far-reaching than was intended. The subsequent history of trade unions and trade-union law has, to a large extent, been a series of disappointments at the failure of the Act to come up to expectations when tested in the courts, and consternation at the effect in law of which it proved to be capable.

Perhaps this is not surprising, for when a statute of this kind, which runs counter to the currents of common law, is introduced into the main stream of law, it is impossible to foresee the eddies and cross-currents that will be set up, and which will cause dislocation and violence in unexpected places. This occurred in spite of the cautious and carefully considered language used by Parliament.

The first provision of the Act of 1871 is a section that was intended to modify the law of conspiracy. It provides that members of trade unions should not be liable to be prosecuted for criminal conspiracy because the purposes of their union are in restraint of trade. Since the Act there has been considerable discussion among lawyers as to whether this section was necessary, and whether in fact it introduced any change in the law. However that may be, it is now beyond doubt that a trade union is permitted to have objects and purposes which are in restraint of trade without its members and officers being liable to be prosecuted for conspiracy.

The Act goes on to extend the protection of the law to the property trusts and agreements of trade unions.

To this end it provides that the agreements and trusts of a trade union shall not be void or voidable because the objects of the union are in restraint of trade. In other words, it makes agreements of trade unions and provisions in the rules of trade unions that are in restraint of trade, legal and unimpeachable.

If this provision had stood alone and unmodified, the courts would have found themselves bound to enforce such contracts directly, by injunction, or by awarding damages for their breach. It may well be that they would have been called upon to enforce strikes and lock-outs by means of an injunction ordering the members of a union to cease work, or an employer to refuse employment to his work-people.

To save the courts from being placed in this position the Act provides that certain agreements of a trade union, although lawful, shall not be directly enforceable, nor shall proceedings be brought to recover damages for their breach. Contracts within this provision are agreements between members as to the conditions on which they shall be employed, agreements for the payment of penalties and subscriptions, agreements between trade unions, and certain agreements for the application of the funds of a trade union, or any bond to secure the performance of such agreements.

The Act then proceeded to make provision for the registration of trade unions, if the members so desired. To qualify for registration the union must have rules in writing which set out the whole of its objects, and make provision for its management, its officers, and the investment and safe keeping of its funds. A registered trade union is required to have a registered office, and to make annual returns to the Registrar of Friendly Societies setting out its property, income, expenditure, and so forth.

Finally the Act defines a trade union. As this definition had unexpected consequences we set it out in full:

'The term "trade union" means such combination, whether temporary or permanent, for regulating the relations between workmen and masters, or between workmen and workmen, or between masters and masters, or for imposing restrictive conditions on the conduct of any trade or business as would, if this Act had not been passed, have been deemed to have been an unlawful combination by reason of some one or more of its purposes being in restraint of trade.'

As a result of this short and guarded statute, the trade union was established as one of the institutions of the industrial world, and, if it chose to register, with something very similar to corporate existence. What before the Act was considered a conspiracy in restraint of trade emerges from the Act as a new form of legal association.

It was not long before defects in the Act began to appear. The first was the definition of a trade union. By restricting the definition to such trade union 'as would, if this Act had not been passed, have been deemed to have been an unlawful combination', the benefits of the Act were conferred only on trade unions which would have been unlawful before the Act. In order to register, the trade union had to satisfy the Registrar that its rules were in fact in restraint of trade. Thus the advantages of registration were offered only to illegal trade unions, and not to those that had avoided illegality.

Next it became apparent that the intended modification of the law of criminal conspiracy had had little or no effect, for although after the Act a strike was not a criminal conspiracy in restraint of trade, it remained, in most cases, a conspiracy to coerce.

This defect in the Act became apparent in November 1872, when a man named Dilley, who was employed by the Gas Light & Coke Company, refused to do work he was ordered to do, on the ground that it was contrary to the rules of his union. His employers dismissed him, and thereupon sixty fellow members of his union struck without notice, and in breach of their contracts of employment. A number of the strikers were tried at the Old Bailey before Mr Justice Brett and a jury, for conspiracy to molest their employers in the conduct of their business. The Judge told the jury that anything done with improper intent to the unjustifiable annoyance of the employer in the conduct of his business, and such as would have a deterring effect on a man of ordinary nerve, is 'molesting', and unlawful. The jury found the men guilty, made a recommendation to mercy, and the accused were each sentenced to twelve months hard labour. The case is known as R. *v.* Bunn, and is reported in 12 Cox at page 316.

Thirdly, the Act gave no protection against the law of civil conspiracy. This is a branch of the common law which had its origin in the Court of Star Chamber, but which developed largely after 1871 because of the increased power and activity of the trade unions.

In the course of a strike, damage is almost inevitably suffered by the employer as a result of the combined efforts of the strikers. The civil law of conspiracy entitled the employer to bring an action against the strikers or their leaders to recover the damage suffered. This was decided in the case of Quinn *v.* Leathem ((1901), A.C. 495). The case arose out of the actions of a Belfast union of butchers' assistants, who tried to enforce a closed shop in the trade.

Quinn was the treasurer of the union. Leathem was a flesher who employed assistants who were not members of the union. Munroe was a butcher who had been in the habit of buying meat each week from Leathem. First the union tried to pursuade Leathem to dismiss his non-union assistants. He refused to do so, but offered to pay any demand the union might make if it would admit his assistants to membership. This the union refused. The union next approached Munroe, and threatened to call out his employees on strike unless he ceased buying meat from Leathem. Munroe complied with this demand, and ceased trading with Leathem.

Leathem thereupon brought an action against Quinn and other officials of the union on the ground that they had conspired together to injure him, and that as a result he had suffered damage. The action was tried by a jury, who found that Quinn and his fellow officials had in fact combined together for the purpose of injuring Leathem, and they awarded him £250 damages. Quinn appealed to the House of Lords, who upheld the jury's award. As a result of this case it was established that if two or more persons combine together, without legal justification, to injure another, and by so doing cause him damage, they are liable in an action for conspiracy.

This decision standing alone would not have been

catastrophic to trade unions, but it did not stand alone. It operated in conjunction with a further unexpected development of the law.

Before 1871 it had been impossible for persons injured by the activity of trade unions to reach the union's funds by any process of law. There was no procedure by which the courts could order that damages suffered should be paid out of those funds. The procedure of the old courts of common law was too rigid. It could not be adapted to actions against unincorporated associations. The result was that the funds of trade unions were 'inviolate'.

About the end of the last century trade unions discovered that this happy and privileged position no longer existed. It came about in this way:

1. The Act of 1871 made provision for bringing actions against the trustees of registered trade unions in any action 'touching or concerning' any right or claim to the property of the union. It was not at first realized how far-reaching this provision was.

2. As a result of the Judicature Act 1873 the procedure of the courts was improved, and it became possible to bring claims for damages against the funds of trade unions by what is called a 'representative action'. It is so called because a few representative members are made defendants, but the judgement binds the whole membership of the union.

3. In the Taff Vale Case ((1901), A.C. 426), the House of Lords held that a registered trade union could be sued in its own name. In August 1900 the Amalgamated Society of Railway Servants called a strike against the Taff Vale Railway Co., and the Company brought an action against the union in its registered name for an injunction to restrain the union, by its officers or agents, from picketing the Great Western Railway Station at Cardiff, and for damages. The

union applied to Mr Justice Farwell to strike its name out of the proceedings on the grounds that unions could not be sued in their own names.

The union was registered, and the court held that as a result of the Act of 1871 a registered union acquired sufficient corporate existence to be sued in its own name. This decision was confirmed by the House of Lords. Subsequently the railway company recovered £23,000 damages from the union.

In these ways procedure became available whereby judgements could be obtained against a trade union that could be enforced against the property and funds of the union.

The combined effects of these blows almost brought trade union activities to a standstill. As a result of Quinn *v.* Leathem any strike might be held to be a conspiracy to injure, for which the employer might be able to recover damages. As a result of the Taff Vale case the judgement for damages could be enforced against the funds and property of the union.

The Act which had been hailed as the trade-union charter had proved to be their undoing. Their existence was now threatened, and the Act of 1871 came to be regarded by most trade unionists as the most oppressive of all the oppressive legislation that had encumbered the growth of trade unions, while the less well informed blamed the courts for having robbed them of the benefits of the Act.

But this was not all. The Act of 1871 produced a further unexpected result. As has already been mentioned, the Act defined a trade union as any combination having specified objects (that is, a combination for regulating the relations between workmen and masters, or between workmen and workmen, or between masters and masters, or for imposing restrictive conditions on the conduct of any trade or business). When this definition came to be considered by the courts it was held that a trade union was not entitled to have any additional objects, and that therefore the collection of funds for political purposes was illegal.

This was decided in Osborne *v*. Amalgamated Society of Railway Servants ((1910) A.C. 87). Osborne was the secretary of the Wolverhampton Branch of the union, and he objected to paying a contribution of 1*s*. 1*d*. a year to the political fund. He brought an action to have the fund declared illegal, and to restrain the union from collecting or expending money on political objects. The action was successful. It was held that the definition of a trade union in the Act was a limiting definition, and that as a result trade unions were not entitled to have any objects in addition to the statutory objects (those mentioned in the definition in the Act), and that the political fund of the society was therefore illegal.

All the foregoing defects in the Act of 1871 were unexpected. They became evident in practice, and were dealt with piecemeal by Parliament. Between 1871 and 1913 four Acts, intended to improve and strengthen the position of trade unions, were passed.

In 1875 the Conspiracy & Protection of Property Act enacted that an agreement by two or more persons to do or procure acts in contemplation or furtherance of a trade dispute shall not be indictable as a conspiracy unless the acts themselves are punishable as a crime. This finally disposed of the menace of criminal conspiracy as far as trade unions and trade unionists were concerned. A principle of the common law which had perhaps been more inhibiting to them than any other single principle was at last rendered harmless. So long as no acts that were themselves criminal were committed, trade unionists were now free to plan and execute 'direct action' in trade disputes and to interfere with the freedom of others without the fear of criminal proceedings for conspiracy being taken against their leaders.

Next came the Trade Union Act 1876. This made a number of minor alterations in the law, and modified the definition of a trade union so as to include unions that were not unlawful at common law.

The third intervention of Parliament took place in 1906, in the Trade Disputes Act of that year. This is an Act of considerable importance. It carried to a logical conclusion the policy initiated in 1871 by giving trade unions a privileged position under the law.

(*a*) It removed the risk to trade unions of an action for damages for civil conspiracy in trade disputes, by enacting that any act done pursuant to an agreement in contemplation or furtherance of a trade dispute should not be actionable as a conspiracy unless the act, if done without the agreement or combination, would be actionable.

(*b*) It gives persons acting in trade disputes immunity from liability for procuring breaches of contracts of employment, or interfering with the trade or employment of some other person. In this way, members of trade unions, be they employers or employees, acting in a trade dispute are free from the liability that ordinarily attaches at law to acts of this kind. Thus the 'lightning strike', called in breach of the contractual obligations of the workmen, became a possible instrument of trade union tactics.

(*c*) The most far-reaching provision of the Act, however, is the immunity given to trade unions from legal proceedings for torts committed on their behalf. As a result their funds cannot be reached in actions against the union itself, or in representative actions, for any tort, be it libel, negligence, or strike activity.

(*d*) Finally, the Act defined a 'trade dispute' as any dispute between employers and workmen, or between workmen and workmen, connected with the employment or terms of employment or conditions of labour of any person.

This act remedied the major shortcomings that had been disclosed in the Act of 1871 and gave trade unions a unique position before the law. The former Acts had attempted to make the activities of trade unions lawful—to put them on a footing of approximate equality with other institutions.

Practice showed that this was impossible. The weapon of the strike and the other coercive activities which in the past have been considered essential for a trade union, could not be fitted into any scheme of equality before the law. In the result the intention of making trade unions lawful led to a new form of privilege.

This statute (the Trade Disputes Act 1906) was passed largely as a result of the political activity of trade unions and trade unionists. In 1900 the Trade Union Congress had joined forces with socialist organizations to form the Labour Representation Committee, which in 1906 was re-named the Labour Party. Some trade unions had adopted political objects, such as the establishment of a socialist state. Many of them had procured the election of their nominees to Parliament. The growing ranks of their members were proving a ready source of funds for political purposes.

It came therefore as a shock to the trade-union movement when in 1910 the House of Lords held, in Osborne's case, that trade unions were not entitled to raise or expend funds for political purposes, and, in effect, that the privileged status of a trade union was not compatible with political activities.

Trade unions mobilized their forces to reverse this judgement. This was achieved by the Trade Union Act 1913.

This Act extends the statutory definition of a trade union by making it more flexible. It authorizes political activities and political objects; but for certain specified types of political activity it requires that a separate political fund be set up. It requires that a union that maintains such a fund should have rules that exempt members who do not wish to contribute from doing so, and from unjust discrimination.

The Act also provides that any person who considers himself aggrieved by a breach of the rules of the political fund shall have a right to complain to the Registrar of Friendly Societies, who can make an order to remedy the grievance. Any such order can be enforced as though it were an order of a County Court.

This Act marks the limit of the statutory evolution of the general law affecting trade unions. Since the Act of 1913 they have grown in stature, in numbers, in power, and in influence. They are now among the most powerful institutions in the state.

Since 1913 there has been trade-union legislation, but in the main it has been of a political rather than a basic nature.

In 1919 there was a police strike. This resulted in the Police Act 1919, which prohibits policemen from belonging to any trade union, but in lieu establishes the Police Federation.

In 1920 there was a strike in the mining industry. This resulted in the Emergency Powers Act 1920, which authorizes the Government to proclaim a 'state of emergency' if it appears that essential services are threatened by action or intended action. Regulations can then be made to procure the continuation of public services, and although the right to strike and peacefully to pursuade others to strike is expressly preserved, any breach of the regulations is punishable by fine or imprisonment, or both.

In 1926 came the General Strike. It led to the passing of the Trade Disputes & Trade Union Act 1927. By this Act two types of strike were made illegal:

1. A strike which had any object other than that of furthering a dispute within the trade or industry in which the strikers were employed.

2. A strike designed or calculated to coerce the Government, either directly, or by inflicting hardship on the community.

Thus sympathetic strikes, or strikes with a political or quasi-political object, were declared illegal.

Secondly, the Act restricted the right to picket.

Thirdly, it varied the rules governing political funds by substituting 'contracting in' for 'contracting out', which meant that before a trade union could collect contributions for the political fund from a member, he had to signify in writing his willingness to contribute. Until this Act a union was entitled to collect contributions from a member until he signified in writing his refusal to contribute. The effect of this change was considerable. There are many members of unions who hold no very strong political views, and others who hold political opinions which are opposed to those of the union. It enabled these classes of members to avoid payment to the political fund by merely doing nothing.

The Act prohibited servants of the Crown from belonging to outside trade unions. It permitted them to form their own unions, but prohibited political objects or association with political bodies or affiliation with outside bodies or federations of unions. It prohibited local authorities and other public bodies from making it a condition of employment that any person should or should not be a member of a trade union. This Act aroused the bitter opposition of the trade-union movement, partly because of the effect it had on their political funds, but primarily because it outlawed the 'sympathetic strike'.

During the last War and the difficult period that followed, the trade unions accepted and supported the Conditions of Employment and National Arbitration Order 1940, which made both strikes and lock-outs illegal until after specified attempts had been made to settle the dispute by negotiation or arbitration.

In 1945, when the Labour Government were returned to power, they immediately introduced legislation—the Trade Disputes & Trade Union Act 1946—which wholly repealed the Act of 1927, and restored the position to what it was before that Act.

In the meantime trade unions have continued to grow in size and in responsibility; in responsibility not only to their members but also to the community in general. They have come to be regarded as indispensable under the conditions of modern industry. Collective bargaining—that is to say, negotiation of wage claims between unions of employers on one side, and unions of employees on the other—has become normal practice.

CHAPTER III

WHAT A TRADE UNION IS

WE are now in a position to attempt to define a trade union. As has been pointed out, there is a statutory definition which was introduced by the Act of 1871 and extended by the Acts of 1876 and 1913. In its final form it is:

'The expression "trade union" means any combination, whether temporary or permanent, the principal objects of which are under its constitution—

(a) the regulation of the relations between—
(1) workmen and masters or
(2) workmen and workmen or
(3) masters and masters or
(b) the imposing of restrictive conditions on the conduct of any trade or business
(c) and also the provision of benefits to members.'

No more than a glance is necessary to realize that this is a definition of great breadth, and that a variety of organizations are embraced by it.

Its limits have not yet been clearly marked by judicial decisions, but in one respect it is wider than it at first appears. It has been held that the provision of benefits to members is not an essential object, but an additional or optional object. This was decided by the Court of Appeal in Performing Rights Society v. London Theatre of Varieties (1922) 2 K.B. 433. In coming to this conclusion the

24

court was influenced by the historical development of the definition in the successive Acts. The effect of the decision is that it is unnecessary for a trade union to have benevolent or provident objects. A combination may be a trade union although it does not provide benefits for its members.

In the result any combination, whatever its form, that has for its principal objects the regulation of the relations between workmen, or between employers, or between workmen and employers, or the imposing of restrictive conditions on the conduct of a trade is a trade union. Many combinations which would not otherwise be trade unions now fall within the definition, such as branches of trade unions, and similar organizations.

Let us look at the definition more closely, and see whether we can reach any conclusions about the nature of the associations that fall within its scope.

The word 'combination' also has great breadth of meaning. Any two or more persons who agree to act in consort form a combination. The word therefore embraces not only associations with formal rules, such as the great registered workmen's trade unions of today, but also any two or more persons acting together for an agreed object. The agreement may be in writing and contained in a book of rules, or it may be an oral agreement made on the spur of the moment, such as an agreement between a group of men in a factory who decide to strike because their wages have been reduced or because a fellow workman has been dismissed. Or the agreement may be implied, for example, where the men in a factory, moved by common indignation, find it unnecessary to put their intentions into words, and strike pursuant to a tacit common agreement. All these are 'combinations'. If, therefore, their principal objects are statutory objects (that is, objects contained in the statutory definition) they would seem to be trade unions.

c

There is no need for the combination to be permanent. Of course, in a great many cases, trade unions are set up with the intention of creating a lasting organization, but this is not necessary. A trade union may be a combination intended only to last for a day, or even less.

To return to the men in the factory: if they decided, because of some grievance relating to the terms of their employment, to down tools for an hour, they would appear to be a trade union for that hour, or so long as they acted in combination for one of the statutory objects.

The Act of 1871 itself, as has already been mentioned, originally applied only to illegal trade unions. Many people at that time considered trade unions to be conspiracies. The word 'combination' in that Act was intended to cover what many would have described as a conspiracy.

In thinking of trade unions, one must always bear in mind that the expression not only applies to the large, wealthy, articulate organizations which usually pass under that name, but also may apply to any two or more men who for a day or longer agree to act together for one or other of the statutory objects.

There is only one test: not the desire of the members, not registration or any other formality; but what are the principal objects of the combination?

If they are statutory objects, the combination is a trade union, however much that result may be against the wishes of the members, and regardless of whether the members have tried, by forming themselves into some other type of association, such as a limited company or Friendly Society, to avoid being a trade union.

Similarly a trade union remains a trade union only so long as its principal objects are statutory objects. To return to the example of the men in the factory. Let us assume that on Monday they form a strike committee in order to strike for higher pay. On Monday, therefore, they are a trade union because they are a combination the principal object of which is a statutory object (that is, the regulation of the relations between workmen and masters). Let us next assume that on Tuesday their demands are granted. They meet to consider their position. They decide to continue their existence in order to assist in a political election that is imminent. Do they continue to be a trade union? The answer is 'No'. The object of the combination has changed and the new object is no longer a statutory object. They have ceased to be a trade union.

Let us next assume that on Wednesday one of their fellow employees is dismissed. The strike committee meets again and decides to call a strike in order to achieve the reinstatement of the dismissed man. The committee now has two objects: (1) a political object and (2) an industrial object which is one of the statutory objects. Has it become a trade union again? The answer depends on which of the two is the principal object. If the principal object is still political it is not a trade union. If, on the other hand, the principal object is a statutory object, it is.

But assume that both objects are equal—that neither can be said to be more important than the other. Neither is first in rank or importance. Is such a combination a trade union? That answer must be that it is not. The protection of the Acts is given only where the combination has principal objects, and those objects are statutory objects.

What has been said of the example of the strike committee applies to all trade unions which are not registered or certified.

If a trade union is registered or certified under the Acts it is presumed to be a trade union so long as it is so registered or certified. It is, however, the duty of the Registrar to cancel the registration or certification if he finds that the combination is being carried on principally for non-statutory objects.

This is the result of Section 2 (2) and (3) of the Act of 1913, which are as follows:

'(2) The Registrar of Friendly Societies shall not register any combination as a trade union unless in his opinion, having regard to the constitution of the combination, the principal objects of the combination are statutory objects, and may withdraw the certificate of registration of any such registered trade union if the constitution of the union has been altered in such a manner that, in his opinion, the principal objects of the union are no longer statutory objects, or if in his opinion the principal objects for which the union is actually carried on are not statutory objects.'

And

'(3) Any unregistered trade union may, if they think fit, at any time without registering the union apply to the Registrar of Friendly Societies for a certificate that the union is a trade union within the meaning of this Act, and the Registrar, if satisfied, having regard to the constitution of the union and the mode in which the union is carried on, that the principal objects of the union are statutory objects, and that the union is actually carried on for those objects, shall grant such a certificate, but the Registrar may, on an application made by any person to him for the purpose, withdraw any such certificate if satisfied, after giving the union an opportunity of being heard, that the certificate is no longer justified.'

The word 'constitution' used in this section and in the definition does not refer to any written document, or formal act. The Acts do not call for a written constitution and there is little that is formal about many trade unions. It would seem that it must mean the manner or way in which the union is made up and carried on (that is, the way in which it is constituted).

It follows that the large registered unions and certified

unions are trade unions only so long as their principal objects remain, to the satisfaction of the Registrar of Friendly Societies, one or more of the statutory objects. If such a trade union alters its rules or practice so that its principal objects cease to be statutory objects—so that in the opinion of the Registrar it comes to be carried on primarily for non-statutory objects—it would be his duty to withdraw the certificate of registration.

Most of the large unions of today are registered. They are composed of a large number of members who are organized into branches, each branch having its own officers and rules. In the eyes of the law, each branch may be a separate union.

The large registered union is therefore not only a union in its own right but is, at the same time, a federation of smaller unions: the smaller unions being branches or other subordinate organizations existing within the parent union.

If one thing emerges more clearly than another it is that Parliament has not attempted to impose a strait-jacket upon trade unions by forcing them into any rigid mould. They are allowed almost unfettered freedom in the form of their organization.

They are also allowed almost unfettered freedom of activity. So long as their principal objects are statutory objects, they may have any other objects they choose, and may apply their funds for any lawful object or purpose which is authorized under their constitution, subject only to this: if they desire to maintain a political fund they must comply with the requirements of the Act of 1913—a subject with which we deal in Chapter IX.

Trade unions can therefore trade or carry on business. They have liberty, in short, to do almost all the things that a natural person can do. Some unions have found it convenient and useful to do insurance business, many publish news-sheets.

The conception of a trade union carrying on a business

undertaking as an employer of labour may not be as far-fetched as it appears. In practice such activities may not be incompatible with trade-union objects. It has been attempted on a large scale in Israel, where the dominant trade union—the Histraduth—has successfully entered the building trade, wholesale and retail trade, manufacture, and transport, and has become one of the largest employers in the country. It finds no incompatibility between its trading objects and its trade-union objects. It is also a political party.

In England, however, a trade union would lose its trade union status if it permitted its non-statutory objects to become more than secondary objects.

In theory, a large registered trade union is in the same position as the small group of men in a factory, who combine for one or more of the statutory objects. If the court or the Registrar declare on Monday that it is a trade union because its principal objects are statutory objects, it could, in theory, cease to be a trade union on Tuesday. In practice, however, such a union is a highly complex organization, handling large funds and governed by a complex code of rules and it could not easily alter its fundamental character.

The trade-union legislation applies to employers' federations in the same way as it does to the trade unions of workmen.

The following organizations have been held not to be unions: a society of composers and publishers founded for the protection of musical copyright, its principal object being to protect its members' rights, and not to impose restrictive conditions on the conduct of their business; an association the principal object of which was to acquire patent rights, notwithstanding that it regulated output and price; an association to promote and protect Liverpool cotton traders, although it also punished members for misconduct in their business.

On the other hand, an association of mineral-water manufacturers formed for the purpose of protecting members' bottles from unauthorized use, and for restricting members in the purchase and exchange of bottles, and in the employment of ex-employees of other members, was held to be a trade union, and its registration as a limited company was held to be void.

In the optional principal object—that is, the provision of benefits to members—the word benefits means such things as sick pay, pensions, disablement benefit, accident benefit, payment for loss of tools, and so forth. Although the payment of such benefits may be a principal object, it cannot be the sole principal object.

In order to ascertain the principal objects of an association neither the court nor the Registrar are bound by the usual statement of objects in the rules. They may look at the whole of the rules—if the rules are in writing—and at the practice and constitution of the association to discover its real objects.

A trade union may not register as a Friendly Society, or as an Industrial and Provident Society, or as a company. Such registration, if effected, is void.

CHAPTER IV

TYPES OF TRADE UNIONS

THERE are many different ways of classifying trade unions. For some purposes they are divided into trade unions of employers and trade unions of workmen. Thus in the Monopolies & Restrictive Practices (Inquiry and Control) Act 1948, different considerations apply to trade unions of employers and trade unions of workers.

For other purposes trade unions are classified into general and craft unions.

The law of trade unions disregards these distinctions, and creates a classification of its own. To borrow the language of natural science, the law creates two distinct species of trade union, and each species has three varieties.

SPECIES I

Trade unions that are lawful at common law.

Varieties

1. Registered trade unions.
2. Certified trade unions.
3. Trade unions that are neither registered nor certified.

SPECIES II

Trade unions that are unlawful at common law.

Varieties

1. Registered trade unions.
2. Certified trade unions.
3. Trade unions that are neither registered nor certified.

32

There is a basic distinction between species I and II. Trade unions that are lawful at common law have the same status as any other lawful association. Their contracts are enforceable, and the union, its property and trusts, enjoy the full protection of the law.

The test of whether a trade union is lawful at common law lies in its constitution (that is, the contract between the members that forms the basis of their concerted action). As we have seen in the last chapter, this contract may be contained in formal written rules, as in the case of the great workmen's unions, or it may be contained in any other informal contract. For the sake of brevity we shall refer to the constitution of a trade union as its rules.

If the rules are wholly lawful at common law, the combination is lawful at common law. If the rules are not lawful at common law, the combination may be a criminal conspiracy, or it may be a trade union of the second species (that is, a trade union that is unlawful at common law). This depends on the nature of the unlawful provision in the rules.

The words 'unlawful' and 'illegal' are unfortunately not precise words. They cover a variety of acts. If an act is criminal it is said to be unlawful. If an act constitutes a civil wrong—a tort—such as libel, trespass, nuisance, it is also said to be unlawful. Similarly there is a class of acts which are called unlawful or illegal because they are against the policy of the law. In this class fall contracts that are in restraint of trade; that is, contracts that impose an unreasonable fetter on a person in the pursuit of his trade or business. Such contracts are unlawful only because they are against public policy, or perhaps it is more accurate to say against the policy of the law.

Their unlawfulness is of a different nature from the unlawfulness of the other classes of acts that we have mentioned. If an act is criminal, it may be visited with a penalty. If an act constitutes a tort, it may create a liability to pay damages which can be recovered in the civil courts. But if an act is unlawful because it is against the policy of the law, the courts will not do anything that may assist the parties in carrying out their unlawful object, but they do not visit the wrong-doer with any penalty or liability to pay damages.

A contract that provides for the performance of an act that is contrary to the policy of the law is unlawful only in this sense: it is void and cannot be enforced.

If the rules of a trade union are in restraint of trade or provide for objects which are in restraint of trade, the union is unlawful in this sense.

If the rules of the combination are unlawful in the sense that they provide for the doing of some act which is criminal or a tort, the combination is a criminal conspiracy (see Chapter V); but if an object of the combination is unlawful only in the sense of being in restraint of trade, then the combination is a trade union of the second species. Such a trade union derives its status, not from common law, but from the Trade Union Acts.

Until the Act of 1871, there was some doubt as to whether such a trade union was not a criminal conspiracy. To resolve these doubts section 2 of the Act provides:

> 'The purposes of a trade union shall not, by reason merely that they are in restraint of trade be deemed to be unlawful so as to render any member of such trade union liable to criminal prosecution for conspiracy or otherwise.'

Until this Act became law the rules of a union that were in restraint of trade, and therefore unlawful, could not be enforced by any legal process, and the contracts and trusts of the union were void. The property of the union was not protected by law.

To remedy this section 3 of the Act provides:

'The purposes of a trade union shall not, by reason merely that they are in restraint of trade be unlawful so as to render void or voidable any agreement or trust.'

From this section most of the large workmen's unions of today derive their legal status and their power to operate under the law. As a result their property is protected by the criminal law; their trusts are valid and can be administered with the assistance of the courts. Their contracts, with the exceptions which we shall consider below, are enforceable.

The difference between the two species of union can be described as follows: if the rules of the union are not in restraint of trade, the union derives its status as a lawful association from common law. If its rules are in restraint of trade it derives its status as a lawful association from the Trade Union Acts, and the courts will protect its property and intervene in its affairs only to the extent to which they have been empowered by those Acts.

WHAT IS UNLAWFUL RESTRAINT OF TRADE

It is the policy of the law of England that a man should be free to exercise any lawful calling as and where he wills. It is also the policy of the law of England that a man of full age and understanding should be free to enter into any lawful contract.

These two principles of the law come into conflict whenever men by their contracts impose a restraint on the free exercise of a trade or business. Many different forms of contract can impose such restraint. For our present purpose we need only consider the rules of trade unions.

As we have pointed out, the rules of a trade union constitute a contract between the members. If, therefore, by their rules a restraint is placed upon how any person carries on his trade or calling, there immediately comes into operation a conflict between the principles of the freedom of contract and of freedom of trade.

Between these two conflicting principles the law seeks to hold a balance. The courts will not interfere with every restraint upon freedom of trade. They will interfere only when men by exercising their freedom of contract impose restrictions on trade which are unreasonable. In each case the question is whether the restraint is reasonable. But what is reasonable from one man's point of view may be unreasonable from another's. The courts have said that in ascertaining whether a restraint of trade is reasonable it must be shown to be reasonable not only from the point of view of the parties to it, but also from the point of view of the public at large.

What is reasonable in this sense? In Horner *v.* Graves ((1831), 7 Bing. 743) Chief Justice Tindal defined it as follows:

'Whatever restraint is larger than the necessary protection of the party can be of no benefit . . . it can only be oppressive, and, if oppressive, it is, in the eye of the law, unreasonable.'

With this in mind, Lord MacNaughton defined the modern principle of unlawful restraint of trade in Nordenfeldt *v.* Maxim Nordenfeldt (1894) A.C. 535, as follows:

'The public have an interest in every person carrying on his trade freely; so has the individual. All interferences with individual liberty in trading, and all restraints of trade themselves, if there is nothing more, are contrary to public policy, and therefore void. That is the general rule. But there are exceptions; restraint of trade and interference . . . may be justified by the special circumstances of a particular case . . . the only justification [is that] the restraint is reasonable in reference to the interests of the parties concerned and reasonable in reference to the interests of the public, so framed and so guarded as to afford an adequate protection to the party in whose favour it is imposed, while at the same time it is in no way injurious to the public.'

This is the test to be applied to the rules of a trade union.

Is the restraint on the freedom of trade such a restraint as is unreasonable in the sense of being oppressive from the point of view of (*a*) the public, and (*b*) the members of the union?

In applying this principle the courts have held that there is nothing unlawful in a rule that empowers the union to 'regulate' the relations between employers and employees, or which authorizes the sanctioning of trade movements for preventing wage reductions or extension of working hours, or for obtaining wage increases, or which make provision for organizing or directing a lawful strike of a voluntary character, or of supporting such a strike.

What is unlawful, however, is any agreement whereby a man agrees to carry on his trade in accordance with the dictates of others: be they the executive, or the majority of the members of a trade union. Any such provision in the rules is unlawful at common law, and a union which has such rules is also unlawful at common law.

This is the basic distinction between the two species of trade unions.

EFFECT OF THIS PRINCIPLE

Until the Act of 1871 the courts had no jurisdiction to intervene in the affairs of an unlawful association.

Section 3 of the Act altered this, and provided, as we have seen, that the contracts and trusts of a trade union should not be void merely because the rules of the union contain provisions that are in restraint of trade. The effect of this section is therefore to extend the jurisdiction of the courts by authorizing them to intervene in the affairs of unlawful trade unions—by authorizing them to administer trusts or enforce contracts which until then were void for illegality.

If this section had stood alone it would have assimilated the position before the law of an unlawful union to that of a lawful one, with the result that the courts would have been bound to enforce contracts in restraint of trade, that is, enforce strikes and lock-outs by injunction or by the award of damages against men for failing to strike, or against employers for failing to lock out their men in accordance with the resolutions of their trade union.

A limit is therefore placed on the jurisdiction of the courts by providing that nothing in the Act shall give the court power to entertain certain proceedings. The limit on the jurisdiction is contained in section 4 of the Act of 1871, and is in the following form:

'Nothing in this Act shall enable any Court to entertain any legal proceedings instituted with the object of directly enforcing or recovering damages for the breach of any of the following agreements, namely:

1. Any agreement between members of a trade union, as such, concerning the conditions on which any members for the time being of such trade union shall or shall not sell their goods, transact business, employ, or be employed.
2. Any agreement for the payment by any person of any subscription or penalty to a trade union.
3. Any agreement for the application of the funds of a trade union:

   (*a*) to provide benefits to members, or
   (*b*) to furnish contributions to any employer or workman, not a member of such trade union, in consideration of such employer or work-

man acting in conformity with the rules or
resolutions of such trade union or
(c) to discharge any fine imposed upon any person by sentence of a Court of Justice or

4. Any agreement made between one trade union
and another or
5. Any bond to secure the performance of any of the
above-mentioned agreements.

But nothing in this section shall be deemed to constitute
any of the above-mentioned agreements unlawful.'

The effect therefore is this: by section 3 the contracts and
trusts of a trade union which is unlawful at common law are
made lawful; but by section 4 the power of the courts to intervene in the affairs of such a trade union is limited. The
limitation takes the form of preventing the courts from entertaining any of the actions mentioned in the latter section.
It was not long before it became apparent that the terms
of this section were not very clear. It was capable of two
possible constructions: a wide construction excluding all
legal proceedings that might have the effect of enforcing any
of the agreements mentioned in the section; or a narrow
construction which would allow any indirect enforcement
other than by means of an action for damages for the breach
of any of the agreements mentioned in the section.
The narrow interpretation has prevailed. This was decided in the case of Yorkshire Miners Association *v.* Howden
(1905) A.C. 256. The union made payments of strike
money in cases not authorized by the rules. Howden, a
member of the union, brought the action for an injunction
to restrain the union from making these payments. By way
of defence the union relied on section 4 of the Act of 1871,
on the ground that the union was unlawful at common law
and the action was instituted with the intention of directly

enforcing an agreement for the application of the funds to provide benefits to members—an agreement mentioned in section 4 (3) (*a*).

The House of Lords held that the action was not brought with the object of directly enforcing one of the recited agreements, but with the object of preventing the misapplication of the funds, and was therefore maintainable.

As a result it is now established that actions that have the effect of indirectly enforcing one of the agreements mentioned in section 4—other than actions for the recovery of damages—are not excluded from the jurisdiction of the courts.

VARIETY I

Registered Unions

Both unions that are lawful and unions that are unlawful at common law can be registered.

There is a basic distinction between registered and unregistered unions. By registration a trade union becomes a quasi-corporation; it acquires attributes of a legal personality. It can sue and be sued in its registered name, and can contract through agents. It does not, however, acquire sufficient legal personality to hold property in its own name, and its property vests in its trustees.

The power to register a union is contained in section 6 of the Act of 1871, and is as follows:

'Any seven or more members of a trade union may by subscribing their names to the rules of the union, and otherwise complying with the provisions of this Act with respect to registry, register such union under this Act, provided that if any one of the purposes of such union be unlawful such registration shall be void.'

In the case of a large trade union with many members, a permanent staff of officers, and with funds to invest and manage, the advantages of registration are very great. Indeed, it is doubtful whether these large organizations could exist without the practical facilities acquired by registration.

A registered trade union can deal in land, and hold property of all kinds in the names of its trustees. It is provided with efficient machinery for the appointment and change of trustees, and for the transfer of its property from one set of trustees to another.

Its members also acquire advantages. As the rules (including any amendments) must be registered, the exact provisions of the rules can be ascertained at any time. Proper accounts must be kept and audited periodically. Persons interested in the funds of the union have a right to inspect its books of account.

Other advantages gained by registration are as follows:

1. The union has greater facilities for bringing and defending legal proceedings.

It can sue and be sued in its own name as though it were a corporation (Taff Vale Ry. Co. *v*. Amalgamated Society of Railway Servants (1901) A.C. 426), and it can sue and be sued by its trustees or other officer under statutory powers.

2. Registration is conclusive evidence that the association is a trade union, and therefore entitled to all the benefits of the Acts.

3. It is entitled to exemption from Income Tax under Schedules C and D in respect of interest and dividends which are applicable solely for the purposes of provident benefits.

4. Members may dispose at death of sums payable by the union and not exceeding £100 by means of a written nomination.

5. Where there is no will and no nomination, the trustees of the union may distribute sums of up to £100 without

D

letters of administration, and for this purpose may treat an illegitimate child as legitimate.

6. The treasurer and other officers are legally bound to render accounts and to deliver up to the trustees all property and effects of the union on being required so to do, and may be compelled so to do by a competent court.

7. There are special summary proceedings for the protection of the funds and property of the union.

8. The union is exempted from the requirements of the Assurance Companies Act 1909, whereby unregistered unions may make themselves liable for heavy penalties.

9. If a trustee is away from the United Kingdom, or becomes bankrupt, lunatic, or dies or has been removed, or if it is not known whether he is alive or dead, stock in public funds held by him on behalf of the union can be transferred by direction of the Registrar.

10. It has a statutory process for changing its name.

VARIETY II

Certified Unions

They may be lawful or unlawful at common law.

An unregistered union may at any time apply to the Registrar for a certificate that it is a trade union. If the Registrar is satisfied, having regard to the constitution of the union and the mode in which it is carried on, that the principal objects of the union are statutory objects, he must grant such certificate. While such a certificate is in force it is conclusive evidence that the association is a trade union and entitled to the protection of the Acts.

The Registrar may withdraw the certificate on the application of any person, after having given the union an opportunity of being heard, if he is satisfied that the statutory objects are no longer the principal objects of the association.

VARIETY III

Unions that are neither Registered nor Certified

They may be lawful or unlawful at common law. All other unions fall into this class. Most of the great unions of today are registered unions, but the majority of present-day unions, of one kind or another, are of this variety: they are neither registered nor certified. The formality of their organization varies; some have elaborate written rules; the constitutions of others may be no more than a temporary agreement. They are combinations of many kinds, the principal objects of which are one or more of the statutory objects.

A trade union that is not registered has no legal personality. Like a club, it is a voluntary association of members, and the law does not distinguish between the association and its members. It cannot enter into contracts that are binding upon persons who may become members in the future. If an officer makes a contract with the authority of the members, it binds the whole membership at the time the contract was made. It follows that a member of an unregistered union is not liable for any debt created on behalf of the union, unless he has authorized the creation of the debt or the rules empower some officer to enter into contracts that bind the members.

For the same reason, members of the executive are in most cases personally liable for debts created by them.

CHAPTER V

COMMON LAW

BEFORE the Trade Union Acts gave unions a privileged position there were numerous aspects of the common law that restrained their activities.

First in place and importance was the tort and crime of conspiracy; second, the tort and crime of intimidation; third, the tort of procuring a breach of contract. The doctrine of restraint of trade and its effects we have already considered.

In this chapter we shall make a cursory survey of these aspects of the common law.

CONSPIRACY

Fear of the crime of conspiracy darkened the days of early trade unionists. First because the penalties were severe, and secondly, because this aspect of the law of England has always been uncertain.

Modern trade-union legislation has removed this threat.

In medieval England conspiracy, as a crime, meant a combination with the object of perverting the course of justice: a form of abuse to which a primitive state is particularly vulnerable.

In Tudor times this crime was expanded by the Court of Star Chamber. At this stage conspiracy was so loosely defined that any agreement which the court disliked on moral or other grounds could be punished as a crime. The crime was complete upon the agreement being made. It was not necessary for any part of the agreement to be carried into effect.

On the abolition of the Court of Star Chamber the common law courts adopted the expanded conception of conspiracy.

The crime was reflected in the civil courts by the tort of conspiracy (that is, a person suffering damage as a result of a conspiracy was given a remedy in the form of an action for damages). The gist of the crime was the agreement to do the unlawful act. The gist of the civil action was that damage had been inflicted by persons combining together for that purpose.

The difference between the crime and the tort was this: the crime was complete as soon as the offending agreement was made; the tort required two additional ingredients: (1) that the object of the conspiracy be carried into effect, at least to some extent, and (2) that a person suffer damage as a result.

The present law of conspiracy developed from these principles. By degrees it has been made more precise, but it still suffers from the serious defect of uncertainty.

It can be defined as follows:

'Conspiracy is an agreement by two or more persons to effect an unlawful object either as an ultimate end or as a means to it.

'The crime of conspiracy is complete as soon as the agreement is made—even though nothing is done in pursuance of such agreement; the tort of conspiracy however requires that some person suffer damage as a result of the agreement.'

One person cannot be guilty of conspiracy; it takes two or more. It was probably the fear of the power of numbers of people acting together that caused the development of the law of conspiracy.

The agreement to effect the unlawful purpose must be a reality. A mere common intention is not sufficient. It is the mutual consent of the parties to the unlawful purpose that creates the crime.

As a matter of practise it is very rarely possible to prove the agreement by direct evidence. It has generally to be inferred from the concerted action of the parties—what lawyers would call 'overt acts'.

The aspect of the law of conspiracy that creates the greatest difficulty is the 'unlawful object', for, as has been pointed out before, 'unlawful' is an ambiguous word.

It includes all crimes, whether they are punishable on indictment or summarily. It includes all torts, including the tort of unjustifiably procuring a breach of contract. It includes 'intimidation'. It includes all acts that are contrary to public decency and morality.

Beyond this, however, lies a border-land of uncertainty, where the unlawfulness does not consist in the act itself, but in the intention with which it is committed. It is now established that where an individual is concerned, an act which is lawful in itself cannot be made unlawful merely because it is committed for a wrongful motive. But where two or more act in concert this is no longer true. Acts which are in themselves lawful may become unlawful because the intention of the parties to the combination cannot be justified.

Thus, the intention of inflicting injury on another person without lawful justification is an unlawful object for a combination. When therefore two or more persons combine for the purpose of inflicting injury on another person without lawful justification they are guilty of conspiracy.

In this field of the law it seems that every new definition creates new difficulties and uncertainties.

What is 'lawful justification'? Or, to put it another way, what motive can justify a combination in inflicting injury on another? To this question no final answer can be given.

The civil law of conspiracy has largely developed since the first of the modern Trade Union Acts, and possibly because of the emergence of large trade unions with potentially great powers to cause injury. It is still too early to attempt a final answer.

On the authorities as they at present stand it would seem that a moral duty can constitute lawful justification.

The law also recognizes that men frequently act not as the result of a single motive, but from mixed and complicated motives. In such a complex of motives' some may be more important than others. Where the predominant motive of those combining is not to cause injury, but to benefit themselves, their combination is not unlawful.

In the case of Crofter Hand Woven Harris Tweed Co. *v.* Veitch (1942) A.C. 435, the officials of a trade union representing the dockers and spinners of the Island of Lewis combined with each other and with mill-owners against certain local producers of tweed cloth. These producers obtained their yarn from the mainland at a lower price than that charged by the island mill owners, and had it woven into cloth by crofters on the island. They were by this means able to sell their finished cloth cheaper than the mill-owners. As a result the mill-owners were unable to agree to a 'union shop' (that is, to employ only union labour, as was desired by the unions).

On instructions from union officials, and without breaking their contracts of employment, the dockers refused to handle the producers' imports of yarn or exports of finished cloth, with the consequence that the producers suffered loss. They brought an action against the officers of the union for damages for conspiring to injure and for an injunction to stop the embargo.

It was held by the House of Lords that as the predominant motive of those combining was the legitimate promotion of their own interests, and the means employed by them were neither criminal nor tortious, the combination was lawful.

INTIMIDATION

Intimidation is any menacing action, or language of a nature that no man of ordinary firmness or strength of mind can reasonably be expected to resist, used with the intent to compel a man, through fear of such menaces, to do something against his will. If damage is caused thereby, it constitutes the tort of intimidation, and the injured party can recover damages by legal proceedings.

Thus if A, by threatening B with harm, compels B to do something whereby he suffers damage, B can recover such damage from A in an action for intimidation. Equally if A by threats compels B to do something whereby C suffers damage, C has a cause of action against A. Quinn *v.* Leathem (see Chapter II) was a case of this variety. Trade-union officials by threats caused a customer to cease trading with Leathem, and he was held entitled to damages from them.

Similarly, where a trade union, in order to force one of its ex-officials to pay a debt, procured his dismissal from successive employers by threats, the union was held liable.

Threats should be distinguished from warnings. There is nothing wrongful in notifying an employer of an intention to do a lawful act. It is otherwise if the threatened action is unlawful.

Thus if an officer of a trade union gives proper notice to an employer terminating workmen's contracts of employment, and at the same time warns him that unless he complies with the union's wishes on the termination of their contracts the men will strike, there is nothing unlawful in the official's conduct. The men are entitled to cease work on giving proper notice, and to tell the employer in advance of their intention is no more than courtesy.

But if the officer tells the employer that unless he complies with the trade union's wishes the men will strike in circumstances that amount to a breach of their contracts of employment, this is at common law an unlawful threat, for the threatened action is unlawful.

PROCURING A BREACH OF CONTRACT

It is also unlawful at common law knowingly to induce a person to break a contract. It matters not what the contract is, provided that the contract itself is not unlawful. Thus to induce members of a trade union to withhold contributions which they are contractually bound to pay under the rules, is actionable.

A moral duty can justify a person in knowingly procuring a breach of contract. Thus to procure a breach of contract with a theatrical manager who paid his chorus-girls so little that they were driven to immorality to supplement their earnings was justified; and a father is justified in pursuading his daughter to break an engagement to marry a scoundrel.

STRIKES AND LOCK-OUTS

At common law strikes and lock-outs are not in themselves unlawful. A strike is a cessation of work by persons employed in trade or industry acting together in a dispute. A lock-out is a cessation of employment by an employer or employers acting in a dispute.

Both strikes and lock-outs can become unlawful if the means employed are unlawful or if their objects are unlawful. If the means or objects are criminal, or tortious, or otherwise unlawful in the sense that we have used the word in relation to the law of conspiracy, the strike is unlawful. Thus if workmen strike in breach of their contracts of employment it is an unlawful strike at common law. So also, if they agree to strike for the purpose of injuring or punishing a fellow employee who has failed to pay a debt due to his union. In these cases the strikes would be conspiracies at common law.

A strike by men for the purpose of benefiting themselves by raising their wages, or for the purpose of compelling their employer to fulfil an engagement entered into with them, or for any other lawful purpose is lawful at common law.

CHAPTER VI

PRIVILEGES

THE privileged position of trade unions before the law has been achieved by inhibiting the jurisdiction of the courts in certain proceedings. In this way an enclave has been formed in the body social where the Queen's writ does not run. In this enclave the trade union is the supreme arbiter, from whom there is no appeal. In this enclave a person may suffer injury as a result of an unlawful act committed by or on behalf of a trade union and yet have no remedy in law because the courts' power to give redress is inhibited by statute.

The enclave is created by three types of privilege:

1. Immunities that attach to trade unions as such.
2. Immunities that attend trade disputes.
3. Modifications of the criminal law.

IMMUNITIES THAT ATTACH TO TRADE UNIONS

1. In the Law of Contract

A number of the large unions of today have provisions in their rules which appear to have the object of making them unlawful at common law. This may well have advantages, because the courts have power to intervene in, and enforce, all contracts of a lawful trade union. If, however, the trade union is unlawful at common law, the courts do not have this power. There is an area where they have no jurisdiction.

The power of the courts is inhibited by section 4 of the 1871 Act, which in effect prevents any action being brought for the purpose of directly enforcing any of the contracts mentioned in the section, or for the purpose of recovering damages for their breach. The reason for and effect óf this provision are considered in Chapter IV.

The contracts affected by the prohibition are:

1. Any agreement between members of a trade union concerning the conditions on which they shall employ or be employed, sell their goods, or transact business.

2. Any agreement for the payment of a penalty or subscription to a trade union.

3. Any agreement for the application of the funds of a trade union: (i) to provide benefits to members; (ii) to make payments to an employer or workman not a member of the trade union in consideration of such employer or workman acting in conformity with the rules or resolutions of the trade union; (iii) to discharge any fine.

4. Any agreement between trade unions.

5. Any bond to secure the performance of any such agreement.

The power of the courts to intervene to protect an injured person in relation to any such contracts is limited. The result is that the power of the trade union is increased, for in relation to any such contract it often has the final word.

By way of illustration assume a member has for years contributed regularly to the funds of a union under rules by which he becomes entitled to weekly benefits on reaching a certain age. If, when he reaches the required age, the trade union refuses to pay, he has no means of enforcing the contract contained in the rules under which his money is due, or of recovering damages for its breach. The courts have no power to intervene on his behalf.

Almost all contracts between members as members, and almost the whole of the rules of a union, fall within the prohibition. In practice it is necessary to examine the facts of each case, first, to see whether the particular contract is one or other of the types of contract mentioned, and, secondly, to see whether the remedy sought is one or other of the remedies that are prohibited.

It has been held, for example, that actions to restrain a trade union from wrongfully expelling a member, or from applying its funds in breach of its rules, are not within the prohibition.

2. *In the Law of Tort*

The inhibition of the jurisdiction of the courts in the case of torts is more extensive. It is contained in sub-section 4 (1) of the 1906 Act and is in the following terms:

> 'An action against a trade union, whether of workmen or masters, or against any members or officials thereof on behalf of themselves and all other members of the trade union in respect of any tortious act alleged to have been committed by or on behalf of the trade union, shall not be entertained by any Court.'

There are two methods of bringing an action directly against a trade union (see Chapter XI). It can be sued in its own name if it is registered, or it can be sued in what is known as a representation action (that is, an action in which representative members or officers are sued on behalf of all the members). This type of action is available whether the union is registered or not. Both these actions are prohibited by the above section. It is therefore impossible to bring an action against a trade union in respect of a tort, and impossible to recover damages from a trade union for a tort, however unlawful the act committed on its behalf may be. Be the act libel, nuisance, or negligence in driving a motor car, no action can be brought directly against a trade union.

It is, however, possible to sue a trade union indirectly. The trustees of a trade union can in some cases be sued in respect of torts touching the union's property. In the case of registered unions, power to sue the trustees is provided by section 9 of the 1871 Act. This right is not affected by the prohibition of sub-section 4 (1) of the 1906 Act, except in respect of tortious acts committed in a trade dispute. The jurisdiction of the courts in actions against the trustees of registered unions is preserved by sub-section (2) of this section, which provides:

'Nothing in this section shall affect the liability of the trustees of a trade union to be sued in the events provided for by the Trade Union Act 1871, s. 9, except in respect of any tortious act committed by or on behalf of the union in contemplation or furtherance of a trade dispute.'

It may be therefore that the prohibition of actions in tort is not as complete as at first appears; and that except in respect of torts committed in a trade dispute there may be a remedy against the trustees of the property of a registered union. This question is considered in more detail in Chapter XI.

An unregistered trade union would appear to have complete immunity in respect of all tortious acts.

IMMUNITIES THAT ATTEND TRADE DISPUTES

Although the term 'trade dispute' had been used in earlier trade-union legislation, it was not defined until the 1906 Act. It is defined by section 5 (3) of that Act as:

'Any dispute between employers and workmen, or between workmen and workmen, which is connected with the employment or non-employment, or the terms of the employment, or with the conditions of labour, of any person.'

The definition embraces (1) a dispute between employer and workman, or (2) between workmen and workmen, which in either case, is connected with (*a*) the employment or non-employment of some person, or (*b*) the terms of the employment of some person, or (*c*) the conditions of labour of some person.

A workman must therefore be a party to the dispute. A dispute between employers alone is not a trade dispute, even though it be connected with the employment or non-employment of a workman, and even though a workmen's union call a strike in furtherance of the dispute.

A personal quarrel or political difference is not a trade dispute. Thus when a trade-union official, in order to force a member of his union to pay a fine or to punish him, procured his dismissal by his employers by threatening that other employees would strike, the dispute was held not to be a trade dispute.

But malicious and spiteful acts committed in contemplation or furtherance of a trade dispute do not lose the protection of the Act because of the motive behind them.

The dispute must have an industrial connexion of a particular kind. It must be connected with the employment or non-employment, or the terms of employment, or the conditions of labour of some person. Thus the dismissal of a union member, or the employment of men who are not union members, or the refusal to employ union members, are all matters connected with the employment or non-employment of some person, and may be the basis of a trade dispute. If, however, there is no dispute with the employer, but merely a dispute as to whether a man should join a particular union, it is not within the definition. But as soon as it becomes a dispute with the employer rather than with the man, it becomes a trade dispute. For this reason, 'closed shop' disputes, 'demarcation' disputes and 'recognition' disputes are in most cases within the definition.

'Terms of employment' means the terms of the contract of employment. So any term of the contract may be the basis of a trade dispute, but not something wholly outside the contract, as for example the division of a bonus (which is in fact a gift) among workmen.

'Conditions of labour' means the physical conditions under which people work, such as light, ventilation, warmth, health precautions, and so on. Any such matter may be the basis of a trade dispute.

Disputes which do not have this particular industrial connexion are not trade disputes. Thus a dispute as to whether or to whom an employer should sell his property, be it aircraft or other goods, is not a trade dispute, nor is a political issue, such as whether an industry should be nationalized.

For the purposes of the definition, 'workman' means all persons employed in trade or industry, whether or not in the employment of the employer with whom the trade dispute arises (section 5 (3) of the Act of 1906). It is therefore not all employees who can be the subject of a trade dispute, but only those who are employed in a trade or industry. Whether employees of the Crown, or of local authorities whose employment is not of an industrial nature fall within the definition is an open question.

It should be particularly observed that the workman need not be in the employment of the employer with whom the dispute arises. As a result 'sympathetic strikes' are within the definition. Therefore action taken by workmen or employers or a person wholly outside the dispute, or even by a mere busy-body, are all equally within the protection of the Act.

The protection given to participants in trade disputes is this:

1. Section 3 of the 1875 Act, as amended by section 1 of the 1906 Act provides:

'An act done in pursuance of an agreement or combination by two or more persons shall, if done in contemplation or furtherance of a trade dispute, not be actionable unless the act, if done without any such agreement or combination, would be actionable.'

The effect of this section is that an injured person cannot rely on the law of conspiracy to recover damages from a person acting in a trade dispute. Thus if persons conspire to injure an employer in the course of a trade dispute, no action will lie unless some independent tort is committed, such as libel, nuisance, assault, or some other wrong which would be actionable if done by a single individual.

The intention behind the section was to over-rule the decision of the House of Lords in Quinn *v.* Leathem (see Chapter II), and, in this object, it was successful.

It is of interest to note in passing that persons acting in concert in a trade dispute, in such a way as to be entitled to the protection of this section, would, it would seem, of necessity, be a trade union (see Chapter IV).

2. The immunity from actions for damages for tort that is given to trade unions by section 4 of the 1906 Act is, in a more limited form, given by section 3 of the same Act to all persons acting in a trade dispute.

The section provides:

'An act done by a person in contemplation or further-ance of a trade dispute shall not be actionable only on the ground that it induces some other person to break a con-tract of employment or that it is an interference with the trade, business, or employment of some other person, or with the right of some other person to dispose of his capital or his labour as he wills.'

At common law it is unlawful to procure a person to break a contract without lawful justification, or to threaten so to do. As a result of this section, if a breach of contract of em-ployment is procured or threatened in the course of a trade

E

dispute, the injured party has no remedy. Thus, if, in the course of a 'closed-shop' dispute, union officials induce an employer to dismiss a workman in breach of his contract of employment, the injured workman cannot sue the union officials to recover the damage he has suffered by their act. His right, however, to bring proceedings against his employer for wrongful dismissal is not affected.

The section has made lawful a potent weapon—one, however, more likely to be used by the agitator than the responsible trade union—the so-called 'lightning strike' (that is, a strike called at a moment's notice and in breach of contract). A demand is made for some immediate concession from an employer, with the threat that if it is not met on the spot, strike action will immediately follow. Such a demand, if skilfully timed, can be very effective.

In some trades it is still possible to bring about a strike of this kind without breaking contracts of employment. These are the trades where labour is still hired, according to custom, on what is called a 'hire-or-fire' basis, and no real notice is required from either side. But in most trades a week's notice on either side is usual. Both the employer and workman are entitled to expect the contract of employment to be honoured. It is in these trades that a 'lightning strike' can have far-reaching effect.

Responsible unions frown upon, and do everything they can to discourage such strikes.

The workmen who break their contracts of employment are not protected by the section. They are liable to their employer in damages, but the procurer or organizer of strikes of this character has been given immunity.

CHAPTER VII

MODIFICATION OF THE CRIMINAL LAW

IN 1871 there was considerable doubt whether a contract which was unlawful because it was in restraint of trade made the parties liable to a prosecution for conspiracy. The matter was of the greatest importance to trade unions, because their rules were frequently in restraint of trade. To clarify the position section 2 of the first of the modern Trade Union Acts, that of 1871, provides:

'The purposes of any trade union shall not, by reason merely that they are in restraint of trade, be deemed to be unlawful so as to render any member of such trade union liable to criminal prosecution for conspiracy or otherwise.'

There is now no doubt that the section was declaratory of the common law, but at the time it had the effect of resolving the doubts and fears of many trade unionists. It did not, however, improve their position or give them any protection that they had not had before. Strikes and other industrial action of the type that had given rise to prosecutions in the past were still unlawful because they were coercive, or were intended to injure some person in his trade or business. The protection they sought was ultimately given them by section 3 of the Conspiracy & Protection of Property Act 1875, as amended by the Act of 1906, which provided:

'An agreement or combination by two or more persons to do or procure to be done any act in contemplation or

59

furtherance of a trade dispute shall not be indictable as a conspiracy if such act committed by one person would not be punishable as a crime.'

This section had the desired effect. Thereafter the fear of being prosecuted for conspiracy ceased to haunt the trade unionist. As is pointed out in Chapter V, the basis of conspiracy is the combination (that is, the agreement for concerted action). This no longer could be the basis for a prosecution in a trade dispute, unless the agreement was to commit some act which was itself punishable as a crime. To combine to commit a tort, or to induce a breach of contract, or to injure a person; all these, if done in contemplation or furtherance of a trade dispute could no longer be made the subject of a criminal prosecution.

PICKETING AND KINDRED ACTS

What acts can be lawfully done by participants in a trade dispute? This has long been a vexed question.

What they want to do is reasonably obvious: to bring the greatest possible pressure on the other side. If they are workmen they chiefly desire to bring the employer's business to a stand-still. They wish to prevent him from getting labour, or the raw materials of his trade, or from selling his products. One way of achieving these ends is to bring pressure to bear on his suppliers and customers by threatening or bringing about strikes in their businesses, as was done in Quinn *v.* Leathem (see Chapter II).

A damaging form of interference is to bring about a failure of his transport arrangements by inducing the employees of his carriers to refuse to carry his goods.

The strikers need to advertise the justice of their cause, and the absence of justice on the side of their opponent, not only by using all the usual means of publicity available to them, but also by picketing the employer's place of business, and possibly the homes of his employees.

They must keep the emotional temperature of the dispute at fever heat, so as to prevent the workers from losing their sense of grievance.

Workmen may take action to bring about all or any of these objects either as individuals or by combined action. Their trade union has civil immunity by reason of section 4 of the Act of 1906. The individual participants have the criminal protection of section 3 of the 1875 Act, and civil protection by section 3 of the 1906 Act. They can bring in outsiders by virtue of the definition of a workman in the Act of 1906. But just how far can they go in interfering with the business or trade of their employer without incurring the risk of criminal prosecution?

There has been considerable conflict of judicial opinion on this subject. The view that emerges from the conflicting decisions seems to be this: interference with the trade or business or private affairs of another is not for that reason only unlawful. There must be some additional element of illegality such as intimidation, nuisance, trespass, fraud, or deceit.

It is obvious that any of the steps which are likely to be taken in support of a strike may easily cross the border-line between what is permissible and what is not.

It is fair and reasonable to try to pursuade a fellow workman to join in a strike. It is improper to threaten him with violence if he refuses. It is permissible to wait outside his house to reason with him when he comes out, but it is improper to wait in such numbers or in such an attitude as to terrify his wife and children.

It is reasonable to picket the employer's place of business to explain to callers why you are on strike, or to pursuade other workmen not to work for him; but fatally easy to do so in such a way that a riot develops.

These questions were dealt with in the Act of 1875. Section 7 of that Act is as follows:

'Every person who, with a view to compel any other person to abstain from doing or to do any act which such other person has a legal right to do or abstain from doing, wrongfully and without legal authority—

(1) Uses violence to or intimidates such other person or his wife or children, or injures his property, or

(2) Persistently follows such other person about from place to place, or

(3) Hides any tools, clothes, or other property owned or used by such other person, or deprives him of or hinders him in the use thereof, or

(4) Watches or besets the house or other place where such other person resides, or works, or carries on business or happens to be, or the approach to such house or place, or

(5) Follows such other person with two or more other persons in a disorderly manner in or through any street or road,

shall on conviction thereof by a Court of summary jurisdiction or on indictment . . . be liable to pay a penalty not exceeding £20, or to be imprisoned for a term not exceeding 3 months.'

To this section, sub-section 2 (1) of the 1906 Act adds an explanatory note in the following words:

'It shall be lawful for one or more persons, acting on their own behalf or on behalf of a trade union or of an individual employer or firm in contemplation or furtherance of a trade dispute, to attend at or near a house or place where a person resides or works or carries on business or happens to be, if they so attend merely for the purpose of peacefully obtaining or communicating information, or of peacefully persuading any person to work or abstain from working.'

This is what is known as 'peaceful picketing'.

It seems probable that both these sections are no more than declaratory of the law as it stood. All the things forbidden by the earlier section would have been unlawful if it had not been passed, and equally 'peaceful picketing' as defined by the latter section probably never was unlawful at common law. The sections have however clarified the position.

It is worth noting that picketing is only authorized in a trade dispute, when either side may do it. But all the offences set out in section 7 of the Act of 1875 can be committed by any person, and for any reason, whether in the course of a trade dispute or not.

The troublesome words in this section are 'intimidates' in sub-section (1), and 'watch' and 'beset' in sub-section (4). None of them is defined in the Act.

The cases decided under the section seem to suggest that all these words involve some threat of personal violence or other unlawful conduct, either express or implied.

BREACHES OF CERTAIN CONTRACTS MADE ILLEGAL

Under the general law any person, employer or employed, who breaks a contract of service is liable in damages to the other party, but he does not thereby commit a criminal offence.

It was early recognized that the legalization of trade unions, with the essential acknowledgement of the right to strike, might lead to strikes in certain public utility undertakings, such as the supply of gas and water, which might inflict great hardship on the public, and even create conditions dangerous to life.

Some modification of the law affecting the duties of the employees of such undertakings was necessary. Parliament did not seek to prohibit strikes in these industries, but prohibited the 'lightning strike' by workmen in breach of their contractual obligations. To this end section 4 of the 1875 Act provides:

> 'Where a person employed by a municipal authority or by any company or contractor upon whom is imposed by Act of Parliament the duty, or who have otherwise assumed the duty of supplying any city, borough, town, or place, or any part thereof, with gas or water, wilfully and maliciously breaks a contract of service with that authority or company or contractor, knowing or having reasonable cause to believe that the probable consequences of his so doing, either alone or in combination with others, will be to deprive the inhabitants of that city, borough, town, place or part, wholly or tò a great extent of their supply of gas or water, he shall on conviction thereof by a Court of summary jurisdiction or on indictment . . . be liable either to pay a penalty not exceeding £20 or to be imprisoned for a term not exceeding 3 months.'

By section 31 of the Electricity (Supply) Act, 1919, this section is extended to persons employed in electricity undertakings, in the same way as it applies to gas and water, and by the Electricity Act 1947, it is extended to the Electricity Boards of the nationalized industry.

The Act of 1875 also contains a much more general provision in section 5, which provides a prohibition of breaches of contracts of service or hiring when such a breach is known, or where there is reasonable cause to believe that such a breach will endanger human life, or cause serious bodily injury, or expose valuable property to destruction or serious injury. The penalties are the same as in the previous section.

This prohibition is general in its application. It is not limited to public-utility undertakings, nor to breaches of contracts of service by employees. It applies equally to breaches by employers.

The illegality aimed at by both sections is the breach of contract. If the contract is legally determined the employees may strike, and the employers may lock-out, no matter how serious the result of such action may be known to be.

CHAPTER VIII

RULES OF A TRADE UNION

THE rules of a trade union constitute a contract between the members. The powers of the union, its officers, its committees, the obligations and rights of its members, must all be found, either directly or by implication, within the four corners of this contract.

If the union or its officers or committees step outside the rules and do acts that they are not authorized to do by the rules, the acts are beyond their powers. Lawyers like to use the Latin phrase and call such acts *ultra vires*.

Although a trade union is permitted to have any lawful object it chooses, the rules must indicate what are the objects and purposes of the particular union. The activities of each union are limited in this way by the objects stated in their rules. Thus if the rules do not authorize the union to run a newspaper it cannot lawfully do so, and a member can restrain the union from so doing by proceedings for an in-
'unction.

Similarly an act may be *ultra vires* a committee. If the executive committee were to attempt to expel a member without having that power under the rules, their action would be *ultra vires*, and could be restrained by injunction. The same principle applies to the officers and meetings of the union.

The rules should limit and define the membership of the union, the method of becoming a member, the persons entitled to join, and the circumstances in which membership ceases. Minors under the age of sixteen and policemen are not entitled to be members of trade unions.

66

If a union is lawful at common law the rules can be enforced in the same way as any other lawful contract. If the union is unlawful at common law it will probably be found in practice that a substantial part of the rules fall within the ambit of section 4 of the 1871 Act, and as a consequence are not directly enforceable, or enforceable by the award of damages. In either case, however, breaches of the rules can be restrained by the courts by injunction, and their interpretation elucidated by declaration.

The rules in force among existing trade unions vary considerably in form and formality. At one end of the scale are the printed books of rules of the large registered unions. At the other end there may be nothing more than a tacit verbal understanding between men who are on strike.

UNREGISTERED UNIONS

An unregistered union need not have rules in writing, or in any particular form. There are no statutory requirements effecting their form or content, except that the principal objects must be one or more of the statutory objects, and if the union has a political fund it must comply with the provisions of the Act of 1913 (see Chapter IX).

In practice, however, it will be found that any trade union that is intended to have anything more than a very temporary life must have rules to govern its affairs, and for record, they must be in writing. In the absence of rules providing for its management, the union can act only by the unanimous agreement of all its members. This is obviously impracticable. If the union is unlawful at common law its rules should set up machinery for calling strikes and for the payment of strike pay. If this is not done the union will not long survive.

In the same way there are no statutory requirements affecting the rules of a certified trade union except those we have already mentioned as applying to other unregistered unions.

To get a certificate, however, the union must satisfy the Registrar that it is a trade union within the meaning of the Acts. In practice he would normally require written rules, for otherwise the question of whether an association were a trade union could only be resolved after a difficult enquiry.

A registered union, on the other hand, must have printed rules, which must deal with the following matters:

1. The name of the union.
2. The place of meeting for the business of the union.
3. The whole of the objects for which the union is established.
4. The purposes for which the funds are applicable.
5. The conditions under which any member may become entitled to any benefit.
6. The fines and forfeitures to be imposed on any member.
7. The manner of making, altering, amending, and rescinding, rules.
8. Provisions for the appointment and removal of:

    (*a*) a general committee of management,
    (*b*) a trustee or trustees,
    (*c*) a treasurer,
    (*d*) other officers.

9. Provision for the investment of funds and for an annual or periodic audit of accounts.
10. Provision for the inspection of the books and names of members by any person having an interest in the funds.

11. Provision for the dissolution of the union.

12. If the union intends to have a political fund it must have rules protecting members who do not contribute to that fund (see Chapter IX).

The rules may, in addition, deal with other matters. Most unions find it convenient to make provision in their rules for a variety of other things, depending on the needs of the particular union.

Any person—not only members—may, on payment of not more than 1*s.*, obtain a copy of the rules of any registered union on application to the head office.

The draftsman who is preparing the rules of a registered union will find some matters with which he need not deal, as they are provided for by the Acts.

1. Section 7 of the 1871 Act gives the union power to deal in land. Such transactions must be in the names of the trustees.

2. Section 8 of the same Act vests the property of the union in its trustees, and gives them control of it, and provides machinery for its transfer on changes of trustees.

3. Section 10 of the same Act limits the liability of a trustee for any deficiency in the funds to the monies actually received by him.

4. Section 11 of the same Act, defines the duties of the treasurer and other officers of the union and requires them to account to the union and its trustees for moneys, securities, books, and papers.

The registration of a trade union is not comparable to the registration of a company. The company does not come into being until it is registered, and the certificate of incorporation issued. A union, on the other hand, must first be created, its rules adopted and printed and subscribed by seven members, who may then submit them to the Registrar, who must satisfy himself that the principle objects of the union are one or more of the statutory objects. If so satisfied he must register the union.

1. Name

A trade union may not be registered under a name identical with or similar to the name of any other registered union, or unregistered union known to the Registrar. A union may change its name at any time with the approval of the Registrar and the consent of not less than two-thirds of its members.

2. Place of Meeting for the Business of the Union

A registered trade union is required to have a registered office to which all communications and notices may be addressed.

This is not necessarily the same thing as the 'place of meeting for business', although in most cases it would be the same. What the statute appears to intend is that the rules should set out the place where the business of the union is normally transacted: where the committee of management and its officers conduct its day-to-day affairs.

3. The Whole of the Objects

On this topic the rules must be exhaustive—they must contain all the objects of the union. For convenience they should be assembled into a single objects clause: but this is not obligatory, and sometimes it is impracticable. The court or the Registrar, in ascertaining the objects of a trade union, are not bound by the objects rule; they are entitled to look at the whole of the rules in order to find out what the true objects are.

A trade union is free to have any lawful objects. The only limitations on this freedom are:

1. In order to qualify as a trade union, its principal objects must be one or more of the statutory objects.

2. It may not have any object which is unlawful.

3. If the union intends to have certain political objects it must have rules for the protection of members who do not contribute to the political fund (see Chapter IX).

4. *The Purposes for which the Funds are Applicable*

A trade union has power (under section 1 (1) of the 1913 Act) to apply its funds in furtherance of any lawful object or purpose for the time being authorized by its constitution. Its rules need not therefore make express provision for such expenditure.

The powers of a trade union would appear to be:

1. Power to do whatever it is necessary to do with a view to attaining the objects and purposes stated in the rules.

2. Power to do whatever else may fairly be regarded as incidental to the stated objects and purposes.

3. Power to do any additional things authorized by the Trade Union Acts.

4. Power to do any additional thing specifically authorized by the rules.

The purposes which it is therefore necessary to mention in the rules are those which are not directly in furtherance of or ancilliary to the objects of the union, such, for example, as the making of charitable gifts, the publishing of a news-sheet, the provision of legal aid to members, and so on.

A union can be restrained by injunction from applying its funds for an unauthorized purpose, or for an unlawful purpose.

5. *The Conditions under which a Member may become Entitled to any Benefit*

The provision of benefits to members is a secondary or optional object. Benevolent objects are not obligatory. If the union has such objects, the rules must set out the full machinery for the collection of funds for and the payment of such benefits. They include such things as accident or disablement benefit, sick benefit, loss of tools compensation, strike pay, burial grants, superannuation benefit, and so on. They probably include non-monetary benefits, such as the use of a convalescent home, or the advice of the union's solicitors and other forms of legal aid.

Many unions spend money on the provision of educational facilities, and these also are probably 'benefits'.

6. *The Fines and Forfeitures to be Imposed on Members*

If the rules of a union do not authorize fines and forfeitures, the union will have no disciplinary power.

The function of exercising disciplinary powers is quasi-judicial, and involves the creation of a domestic tribunal. This subject is considered in Chapter X.

The rules that authorize the imposition of fines and forfeitures should be unambiguous and reasonable, so as to be understood by all the members. The procedure laid down should be simple, for practice has shown that unless the rule can be easily understood, the union may find great difficulty in making valid use of the power.

Forfeitures would seem to include suspension or expulsion of members.

7. *The Manner of Making, Altering, Amending, and Rescinding Rules*

Unless the rules contain provision for their alteration, they can be altered or amended only by the unanimous consent of all the members. This in practice would in most cases be impossible.

Any amendment which is not made in strict conformity with the rules is invalid.

A registered trade union should register alterations of its

rules with the Registrar, although there is no specific requirement to do so in the Acts.

A copy of the rules in force, however, must be sent to the Registrar with each year's annual return. A valid alteration takes effect from the date it is made.

The adoption of a political fund requires special procedure, which is dealt with in the next chapter.

8. Provision for the Appointment and Removal of (a) General Committee of Management

A trade union cannot act in person. It can only act through agents. Its principal agents are the committee of management—sometimes called its executive committee or council. In a registered union their position is roughly analogous to that of the directors of a limited company. In an unregistered union their position corresponds to that of the committee of management of a club.

The Acts place no specific duties on this committee.

A member of the committee, like any other agent, can resign at any time unless he is prohibited from so doing by the rules. The Acts only require the rules to make provision for their appointment and removal, and these requirements apply only to the general committee of management. They do not apply to area or branch committees. Unions will, however, find it desirable to make express provision in the rules for the nomination, election, removal, and duties of all committees that exercise any powers on their behalf.

A minor cannot be a member of the committee of management.

(b) Trustees

The powers and duties of trustees are given more particular attention in the Acts.

1. All the property of the union must be vested in the trustees. The property of any branches must be vested in

F

the branch trustees if there are any, or in the trustees of the union if the rules so provide. Neither the union nor a branch can themselves hold property.

2. The trustees must have the control of the funds and property. Although they generally follow the directions of the committee of management, the trustees must themselves see that there is no misapplication of the funds, even on the express instructions of the executive.

3. They can bring and defend all legal proceedings affecting the property or funds (see Chapter XI).

4. They can call on the treasurer and other officers to account for any moneys and other property of the union in their hands.

5. They must cause the accounts of the union to be audited.

6. In addition they have all the general powers and duties of trustees.

The Acts call for the appointment of a trustee or trustees, but it would be unwise for a union to appoint only one trustee.

Like other trustees, their decisions must be unanimous. They cannot act by a majority.

(c) *A Treasurer*

The treasurer may also be the secretary, but not a trustee, for his duty is to account to them. This duty he shares with all other officers.

The Acts do not provide any other specific function for him.

He should be the chief financial officer of the union, and the rules should define his duties.

(d) *Other Officers*

The only other officer that a union must have is a secretary. He may also be treasurer.

In practice unions normally have other officers such as a president, organizers, and the administrative staff. The branches and areas also have their own officers.

The functions of all these should be defined in the rules, unless they hold office, not as members of the union, but as paid employees.

9. Provision for the Investment of Funds and for an Annual or Periodic Audit of Accounts

The Acts contain no requirements affecting the nature of the securities or property in which a trade union can invest its funds. Unless the rules make some provision, the trustees would be limited to the very narrow range of investments provided for by the Trustee Acts, and which are known as 'trustee securities'.

The rules may give the trustees wider powers of investment, so as to secure a higher return on the funds. They should, however, be in terms that restrict speculative investment.

In practice the audit must be made annually, for the union has to make an annual audited return to the Registrar.

10. Provision for the Inspection of the Books and Names of Members by any Person having an Interest in the Funds

The rules should make the books available for inspection at reasonable times by all persons having the right to inspect them. This right cannot be limited to members, but must include any other persons having an interest in the funds, such as a nominee of a member entitled to some benefit under the rules. The books referred to are all the books of account, and a person entitled to inspect can do so by an agent. The right to inspect the names of members does not include their addresses.

11. Provision for Dissolution

The Acts require that the rules make provision for the dissolution of the union. This means that they must lay down the machinery applicable if the association is ever dissolved.

In the absence of other provision in the rules a union can only dissolve itself by the unanimous consent of all its members and the assets would be realized and divided equally among the members.

12. Political Fund

This subject is dealt with in Chapter IX.

Before leaving the subject of the rules there are three matters about which something must be said.

1. *Legal Aid*

The draftsman of the rules must remember that unjustifiably to assist a person in the prosecution of civil proceedings is an indictable misdemeanour known as maintenance. If a person suffers damage as a result, it becomes, in addition, a civil wrong for which he can recover damages.

Maintenance can be justified on the following grounds: (1) charity; (2) common interest in the subject-matter of the proceedings; (3) that the proceedings threaten the trade interests of other members of the union. It is on the last-mentioned ground that a union can properly assist its members in proceedings arising out of a contract of service, such as wrongful dismissal, negligence or breach of duty arising out of such a contract. It can also assist a member to fight an action if it will save some call by him on its funds. The principle, however, does not cover actions for libel or slander, even if the member is defamed in his capacity as a union official.

2. *Voting Rights*

The common law provides some useful rules on the question of voting rights in bodies where the rules are silent. All questions arising at a general meeting can in the first place be decided by a show of hands. This is a rough-and-ready way of taking the sense of the meeting, but almost an invariably inadequate means of testing the wishes of the whole constituency of the union. The common law therefore provides that any member may demand a poll. This right can only be excluded by provision in the rules. When a poll is demanded it is the chairman's duty to grant it and to fix a time and place for taking it. The meeting continues, in law, until the poll is completed, even though the chairman refuse to grant a poll. The chairman is not entitled to close the poll while voters are still coming in. To exclude a person entitled to vote may invalidate the poll.

In the absence of provision in the rules there would appear to be no power to take a poll by postal ballot or by other voting papers.

A ballot means a secret vote. If therefore the rules provide for a 'ballot' with no qualification, the identity of each voter must be secret. If the voting papers are numbered, so that the officials of the union can find out how members voted, the ballot is invalid.

Most unions require postal ballots for many purposes. The cost of a secret ballot, in many such cases, would be prohibitive. The rules should therefore be carefully drawn so as to hold the balance between the desirability for an inexpensive vote and the desirability for a secret vote.

Mere informality will not invalidate a vote, provided that the procedure laid down in the rules is substantially followed.

3. *Irregularities*

It is not always possible to prevent irregularities occurring. By an irregularity we mean something which is not done in strict accordance with the rules. Such irregularities will occur from time to time in the best and most conscientiously managed unions.

In order to prevent trivial irregularities leading to litigation, the law has adopted the following rule: if the irregular act can be done by a simple majority under the rules, and there are no procedural requirements intended to protect a minority, then the court will not interfere at the suit of a single member, or a minority of members. In other words, if the act is within the powers of the union and can be legally done by a simple majority of the members, then that majority are the only persons who are entitled to complain that the thing they are entitled to do has been done irregularly. This is called the rule in Foss *v.* Harbottle. It applies to registered trade unions, and probably to all unions.

The rule does not apply to an irregularity which amounts to an invasion of the rights of an individual member, such as a refusal to record his vote.

It does not apply to an irregularity that amounts to a fraud on a minority. In such a case the rule is relaxed in favour of the aggrieved minority.

The rule has no application where the irregular act is one that cannot be lawfully done, for any reason, by a simple majority of the members.

CHAPTER IX

POLITICAL ACTIVITIES

THE Trade Disputes Act 1906 was enacted largely as a result of the political activities of the trade unions. It therefore came as a serious set-back to the movement when the House of Lords in 1910 held that trade unions were not entitled to conduct political activities, or collect funds from their members for political purposes. This was the result of the decision in Osborne's case (see Chapter II).

The movement mobilized its forces to reverse this decision. They succeeded in three years by the passing of the Trade Union Act 1913.

The Act extends the definition of a trade union, which had been: 'Any combination, whether temporary or permanent, for regulating the relations between workmen and masters, or between workmen and workmen, or between masters and masters or for imposing restrictive conditions on the conduct of any trade or business.' In Osborne's case this was held to be an exhaustive definition and a trade union was therefore not entitled to have any additional objects.

The new Act starts in this manner: 'The fact that a combination has under its constitution objects or powers other than the statutory objects . . . shall not prevent the combination being a trade union.' So much for Osborne's case.

The Act then proceeded:

1. To re-define trade unions as any combination the principal objects of which are statutory objects.

2. To authorize unions to apply their funds (subject to the provisions of the Act as to political objects) for any legal purpose authorized by its constitution.

3. To require trade unions that decide to expend money on specified political activities to make such expenditure only out of a 'political fund'.

4. To require trade unions that desire to have a 'political fund' to take certain procedural steps to ensure that the fund can only be established if a majority of the members are in favour.

5. To require any union with a 'political fund' to have rules protecting non-contributing members.

The Specified Political Activities

It is not all political activities that are affected by the Act; only the expenditure of money on any of the following:

'(a) on the payment of any expenses incurred either directly or indirectly by a candidate or prospective candidate for election to Parliament or to any public office before, during, or after the election in connexion with his candidature or election; or

'(b) on the holding of any meeting or the distribution of any literature or documents in support of any such candidate or prospective candidate, or

'(c) on the maintenance of any person who is a member of Parliament or who holds a public office, or

'(d) in connexion with the registration of electors or the selection of a candidate for Parliament or any public office, or

'(e) on the holding of political meetings of any kind, or on the distribution of political literature or political documents of any kind, unless the main purpose of the meetings or of the distribution of the literature or documents is the furtherance of the statutory objects.'

'Public office' as used in the section means: 'the office of member of any county, county borough, district or parish council, or board of guardians, or of any public body who have power to raise money either directly or indirectly by means of a rate'.

Political activities that do not involve the expenditure of money on any of the specified activities are wholly unfettered, and do not fall within the restrictions of the Act; but the specified activities seem to cover most political activities.

They are wider in relation to the candidature or election of a candidate or prospective candidate to any of the offices mentioned than in relation to other political activities. At elections all meetings and literature must be paid for out of the political fund. At other times, if the main object of the political meetings or literature is one or other of the statutory objects, then the expenditure can be met out of the general fund.

CREATION OF THE POLITICAL FUND

There are two conditions precedent to the setting up of a political fund.

1. The specified political objects must be approved as objects of the union by a ballot vote of the members held under rules to be approved by the Registrar.

2. The union must adopt rules providing for the keeping of a separate political fund; and for the exemption of members who do not wish to contribute, and for the protection of the interests in the union of non-contributing members.

The practical steps, therefore, that a union must take in order to have a political fund are as follows:

1. It must adopt rules for holding a ballot for the purpose of approving the specified political objects as objects of the union.

2. These rules must be approved by the Registrar, and he must not approve them unless he is satisfied that every member has an equal right, and so far as is possible, a fair opportunity of voting, and that the secrecy of the ballot is secured. The Registrar has prepared model rules for this purpose that can be adapted to the needs of various types of union. He recommends that the union should submit the rules it proposes to adopt to him for approval before adopting them, in order to avoid the difficulty that would follow from adopting rules and then failing to obtain his approval.

3. The ballot must be held in accordance with the rules, and a majority of those voting must be in favour of a resolution adopting the specified political objects as objects of the union.

4. The union must adopt rules, to be approved by the Registrar, providing for the setting up of the political fund, the exempting of members 'contracting out', and for the protection of such members. The statutory requirement is contained in section 3 (1), and is as follows:

'. . . unless rules, to be approved whether the union is registered or not, by the Registrar of Friendly Societies are in force providing:

'(*a*) that any payments in furtherance of these objects [that is the specified political objects] are to be made out of a separate fund (in this Act referred to as the political fund of the union); and for the exemption in accordance with this Act of any member of the union from any obligation to contribute to such a fund if he gives notice in writing in accordance with this Act that he objects to contribute; and

'(*b*) that a member who is exempt from the obligation to contribute to the political fund of the union shall not be excluded from any benefits of the union, or placed in any respect either directly or indirectly under any disability or at any disadvantage as compared with other members of the union (except in relation to the control or management of the political fund) by reason of his being so exempt, and that contribution to the political fund of the union shall not be made a condition for admission to the union.'

The obligation to have the required rules in force is absolute. Approval of the rules by the Registrar is an administrative act, and a nullity if the rules are in fact not in accordance with the statutory requirements. As a result a political fund collected and maintained at a time when the rules of the union are not in accordance with these requirements is an unlawful fund, and the court will restrain the union from collecting, using or maintaining such a fund.

In Birch *v.* N.U.R. ((1950) Ch. 602) the union had a rule which rendered any non-contributor to the political fund ineligible for any office involving control of the political fund. The rule had been approved by the Registrar. The office of chairman of a branch was one that involved control of the general funds and activities of the branch and also of the political fund. Birch, a duly elected branch chairman, was a non-contributor, and on this ground was removed from office by the union. The Registrar having failed to give him relief, he brought an action for a declaration that he had been unlawfully removed from office, and for an injunction to restrain the union and its trustees from either collecting subscriptions for or expending any money from the political fund. Mr Justice Dankwerts held that the fund was an unlawful fund, and granted an injunction and declaration accordingly. The injunction was suspended by the consent of Birch, to enable the union to put its affairs in order.

A member who considers himself aggrieved by a breach of any of the political fund rules is given a special remedy. He may complain to the Registrar, who hears both the complaining member and the union. If he considers that a breach of the rules has been committed, he may make an order for remedying the breach, and his order can be recorded and enforced as though it were an order of a County Court. The order is conclusive, and there is no appeal from it.

No penalties are provided for failure to observe the provisions of this Act. It may be that Parliament considered that the illegality of any political fund collected and maintained in breach of the Act would be a sufficient deterrent.

A member who does not wish to contribute to the political fund may give the union notice in a statutory form to that effect, and from the first day of January next after the notice is given he becomes exempt from the political levy so long as his notice is not withdrawn. This procedure is what is known as 'contracting out'.

By the Act of 1927 'contracting in' was substituted for 'contracting out'; that is, a member need not contribute to the political fund unless he gives notice of his desire so to do. This provision of the 1927 Act was resented by the trade unions, and, with all the other provisions of that Act, it was repealed by the Act of 1947, and 'contracting out' is now the rule.

The dispute as to the relative fairness of the two systems is still hotly debated. 'Contracting out' has proved to be much to the financial advantage of the political funds. It seems that the average member takes the line of least resistance. If he has to do a positive act to contract out, he would rather pay.

In concluding this chapter it may be helpful if we summarize the rules that a union with a political fund must have:

1. It must have its general rules. If it is a registered union these must be registered and comply with the Acts. If the

union is not registered the general rules may be in any form that the union desires and need not be in writing.

2. It must have the special rules for holding the ballot to adopt the political objects. Whether the union is registered or not these must be approved by the Registrar. They must therefore be reduced to writing. As these rules serve one purpose only, they are not usually included in the printed rules of the union.

3. A resolution must be in force approving the furtherance of the specified political objects as an object of the union.

There is no need to include this resolution in the printed rules of the union, as by section 3 (4) of the Act of 1913 'a resolution under this section approving political objects as an object of the union shall take effect as if it were a rule of the union and may be rescinded in the same manner and subject,to the same provisions as such a rule'.

4. The union must have the special rules, considered in this chapter, which are generally known as the 'political fund rules'.

Whether the union is registered or not these rules must be in writing, and must be approved by the Registrar.

CHAPTER X

DOMESTIC TRIBUNALS AND DISCIPLINARY POWERS

A TRADE UNION has no common-law right to fine, suspend, or expel a member. It can, however, acquire such a right contractually (that is, by its rules).

If the rules are silent on these matters the union has no power to take disciplinary action of any kind. If the rules are not silent the union has only the powers given by the rules, and no more. When the rules contain powers of amendment the union can give itself disciplinary powers by an amendment of the rules made in accordance with the requirement of the rules.

Disciplinary powers involve some form of tribunal to administer them: usually a committee of the branch, or a full branch meeting, with rights of appeal to the executive of the union, or to a special committee set up for the purpose.

The rules conferring disciplinary powers should be drafted with great care. They must be clear and unambiguous, for a heavy burden rests on the domestic tribunals of a trade union.

The tribunal must first construe the rules correctly. Having done so, it must act in accordance with their provisions, and in accordance with the principles of natural justice; and it must not exceed the powers conferred upon it by the rules.

If the tribunal fails in any one of these duties the proceedings are a nullity, and the courts will interfere by injunction, and possibly by an award of damages, for the protection of the aggrieved member.

86

The court's jurisdiction over the proceedings of a domestic tribunal of a trade union is based on two conflicting principles:

(1) the courts of law will not permit persons by contract to oust their jurisdiction;

(2) freedom of contract should not be unduly limited.

Between these two principles the law seeks a balance—attempts to 'assess the considerations viewed from the stand point of public interest which tend in one direction with those which tend in another, and weigh them in the balance'.

Any attempt in the rules to prevent the courts from intervening is, therefore, an attempt to oust their jurisdiction, and is invalid. Thus a provision that the executive committee should have the sole right of interpreting the rules is void, so is a provision prohibiting a member from raising a defence of illegality, or fraud, or any attempt in the rules to exclude the principles of natural justice.

The rules frequently provide for appeals from one domestic tribunal to another. To require a member to obtain the decision of the appellate tribunal before commencing an action at law is not an attempt to oust the jurisdiction of the courts. Such a requirement of the rules will be enforced, and premature proceedings in the courts stopped.

If the rules do not expressly require an appeal to a higher domestic tribunal before commencing an action at law, an aggrieved member need not appeal before starting an action to redress his grievance.

It would also seem that even if the rules require an appeal as a condition precedent to an action at law, an aggrieved member need not pursue such appeal before commencing proceedings if the decision of the domestic tribunal is a nullity, so as to lack the quality of a decision; as, for example, if the tribunal is wrongly constituted.

Many of the cases dealing with domestic tribunals have arisen out of disputes in social clubs. The courts have always shown a reluctance to interfere in matters that are purely social in nature, as opposed to matters affecting property or a man's livelihood. They will obviously not show the same reluctance to intervene in the affairs of the domestic tribunals of trade unions, for a man's liberty to earn his living may be at stake. Indeed, they will be alert to protect the rights of a member and to see that their jurisdiction is not interfered with by the rules of the union.

The powers of the tribunal must be exercised in strict accordance with the rules. Failure so to do invalidates their decisions. Thus, if the rules require a specially convened committee meeting, an ordinary meeting is not sufficient. When a certain number of days notice is required by the rules, a lesser number will not do. Notice of the meeting must be sent to every member entitled to be present, unless he is physically incapable of attending. If the rules require written notice of the charge, failure to give notice in writing will nullify the proceedings.

A decision that is unreasonable or contrary to the evidence is an indication that the tribunal has misconstrued the rules.

The powers of the tribunal must be exercised in accordance with natural justice. Lord Justice Morris recently said, 'There is no magic in the phrase "natural justice". When we use it I think we denote no more than what would be regarded as fair and just and seemly and sensible by an ordinary, reasonable, well-disposed, well-informed and impartial citizen.' In other words, the principles of fair play and good faith.

Thus, the member must be given proper notice of the charge he has to meet. He must receive it in time to prepare his answer. He must be given a fair and adequate opportunity of defending himself. The tribunal must not prejudge the case, or act on evidence heard in the absence of the accused member. They should confine their inquiry to matters that are relevant to the charge.

The tribunal need not follow strictly judicial procedure or exclude evidence because it would not be admissible in a court of law, for a domestic tribunal has no power to administer an oath, or to compel the attendance of witnesses or the production of documents.

It must exercise its powers in good faith, for the benefit of the union, and not for any indirect or improper motive.

The courts are not directly concerned as to whether the decision of a domestic tribunal is reasonable. But a decision which is unreasonable or absurd, is some evidence of want of good faith, just as it may be evidence that the rules have been misinterpreted.

It is sometimes said that the courts have no jurisdiction to interfere in the affairs of a domestic tribunal unless some property right is involved. This is a consideration of importance in actions relating to social clubs. The decisions of the tribunals of trade unions always involve some property right, for the rules themselves constitute a contract, and any breach of the rules is an invasion of the property in that contract.

The decision of a domestic tribunal may be as far-reaching as any order of a High Court judge. If the union operates a closed shop, expulsion from the union may mean utter ruin to the member.

REMEDIES AVAILABLE TO AN AGGRIEVED MEMBER

A member who is aggrieved by a decision of a domestic tribunal of his union can bring proceedings in the courts:

(1) for a declaration of his rights;
(2) for an injunction to restrain the union its officers and servants from acting in breach of his rights;
(3) for damages.

G

The question of when and from whom damages can be recovered by an expelled member presents difficulties. Against whom should the claim be made? Against the members of the tribunal? If under the rules the aggrieved member can establish that there is a contract between himself and the members of the tribunal, and can show that the tribunal acted in breach of the contract, he should be able to recover damages from them. So far as we know, no attempt has ever been made to recover damages from the members of a disciplinary tribunal of a trade union.

Against the trade union? Here there are theoretical difficulties. The question of whether a member who is wrongfully expelled from a registered union can recover damages from the union itself is at present the subject of an appeal to the House of Lords (Bonsor *v.* Musicians Union ((1954) 2 W.L.R. 687). In the earlier case of Kelly *v.* National Society of Operative Printers' Assistants (1915) 84 L.J.K.B. 2236, a member of a registered union was wrongfully expelled by the executive committee. He brought an action for an injunction and damages against the union in its registered name. He succeeded in his claim for an injunction, but the Court of Appeal held that he could not recover damages for two reasons: (1) that as his expulsion was *ultra vires* (that is outside the powers of the committee), the committee, in purporting to expel him, were not acting as agents of the union; (2) that as a registered union does not have complete corporate existence, the executive committee were the agents of all the members including the plaintiff, Kelly, so that his suit for damages was in effect a claim against himself.

Neither of these grounds is very satisfactory. They arise out of the conception of a registered union as a quasi-corporation; that is, as having some of the attributes of a legal personality and at the same time being no more than a name for all the members of the union collectively.

The difficulties seem to be procedural only. They would not necessarily arise in a properly constituted representative action or in an action against the trustees of the union—see Chapter XI.

Kelly's case is also unsatisfactory from other points of view. It is probable that the law was never properly argued, for the Court of Appeal overlooked the fact that if Kelly was not entitled to damages, the County Court (from which the case was on appeal) had no jurisdiction to hear the case at all. The Court of Appeal, however, now considers itself bound by Kelly's case, and it can only be overruled by the House of Lords.

Be this as it may, the question is probably not of much practical importance, for a wrongfully expelled member of a union would seem to have a right to recover damages from the executive committee or other officers who exclude him from the union and in practice the union would probably find itself bound to pay damages awarded against its officers.

CHAPTER XI

ACTIONS BY AND AGAINST TRADE UNIONS

THE procedural difficulties in all legal suits by or against trade unions are considerable. These difficulties do not arise from any rule of procedure or logic, but from incidents and accidents in the history of modern trade-union legislation. Before dealing with the law as it stands today we propose to review briefly the essential stages in its development.

BEFORE 1871

Until the Act of 1871 most trade unions were unlawful because their rules were in restraint of trade. They could neither sue nor be sued. This involved both advantages and disadvantages. The advantages were that the courts would not intervene in their internal affairs and because of procedural difficulties their funds could not be reached by any legal process to satisfy any claim arising out of their activities. The disadvantage was that their funds and other property were not protected by law. They could not seek the assistance of the courts to administer their trusts, or enforce their contracts, or preserve their property. It was largely to remedy this position that the trade unions of the day sought a statute that would bring their funds under the aegis of the law.

There were also lawful unions. These were unions with rules that were not in restraint of trade. They were lawful unincorporated associations, and as such enjoyed a somewhat privileged position. Their funds could not be reached in any proceedings in a common law court. This was because at that time the rules of procedure were too rigid. It was therefore impossible to recover a judgement for damages against a union. At the same time they could protect their trusts by suits in equity, because the rules of the old Court of Chancery had been adapted to meet the difficulties created by unincorporated associations.

THE ACT OF 1871

The Act of 1871 did not originally apply to lawful unions, it was made applicable to them by subsequent amendment.

Trade unions that were unlawful were brought under the wing of the law by this Act, which created two varieties of union, registered and unregistered. Certified unions did not come into being until 1913.

The position of the unlawful unregistered union was assimilated to that of the lawful union (that is, it became a lawful unincorporated association).

Registered unions acquired a new status. They became quasi-corporations, empowered to sue and be sued in their registered names. They were also empowered to sue and be sued in the names of their trustees, or by some official designated in the rules.

The Act therefore created three methods of bringing legal proceedings by or against a registered trade union:

(1) in its registered name;
(2) in the names of its trustees;
(3) in the name of any officer designated in the rules.

Section 4 of the Act limited the matters in respect of which proceedings could be brought (see Chapters III and VI).

So long as this Act applied to unlawful unions only, section 4 did not create any confusion. When, however, the Act was extended to lawful unions in 1876, a curious anomaly arose, in this way: all the contracts of a lawful union can be enforced, be it registered or not, but the new methods of procedure provided by the Act of 1871 cannot be used in proceedings that fall within section 4 of that Act, be the union lawful or unlawful at common law.

JUDICATURE ACT 1873

The next step was the Judicature Act 1873. As a result of this Act procedure that had only been available in the old Court of Chancery became available in all the Divisions of the High Court. It became possible to reach the funds of trade unions in actions at law by two new methods:

(1) by representative actions, that is actions against representative members sued on behalf of all the members;

(2) by actions against trustees on behalf of the trust property and as representing the members.

The result of the foregoing procedural developments was so great that trade union activities practically ceased until the Act of 1906 restored to the funds of trade unions some of the immunities they had previously enjoyed.

ACT OF 1906

This Act prohibits any action in tort against a trade union in its own name—a form of action that can only be brought against a registered union—or by means of a representative action—a form of action available against any union.

The Act expressly preserves actions in tort against the trusteees of a trade union under section 9 of the 1871 Act—a form of action that can only be brought against a registered union—except in respect of torts committed on behalf of the union in contemplation or furtherance of a trade dispute.

As a result of these accretions to the law, actions can be brought by or against trade unions in five different ways. Each is subject to exceptions.

1. All trade unions can sue or be sued in representative actions under the Rules of the Supreme Court.

2. The trustees of all trade unions can sue or be sued on behalf of and as representing the union's property vested in them under the Rules of the Supreme Court.

3. Registered unions can sue or be sued in their registered names.

4. The trustees of a registered union can sue or be sued under section 9 of the 1871 Act in all matters touching the property or any right or claim to the property of the union.

5. An officer of a registered union authorized by the rules can sue or be sued under section 9 of the 1871 Act in similar circumstances.

1. REPRESENTATIVE ACTIONS

This is a form of procedure adapted from the old Court of Chancery which is now available in all the Divisions of the High Court; it is set out in Order 16, Rule 9 of the Rules of the Supreme Court.

It is more suitable, as a method of procedure, for the establishment of rights in property than in common law claims for damages or for the recovery of money. The courts have found great difficulty in applying the rule to actions for damages. The trouble arises because in actions for breach of contract or tort a person is only liable for his own actions or those of his agents. In principle, therefore, there may be different defences open to each member of a union.

Since the Act of 1906 the courts are prohibited from entertaining a representative action in respect of a tort committed by or on behalf of a trade union. This prohibition is not restricted to acts committed in a trade dispute.

2. ACTIONS BY OR AGAINST TRUSTEES UNDER THE RULES OF THE SUPREME COURT

This form of procedure, which is governed by Order 16, Rule 8 of the Rules of the Supreme Court, is available against the trustees of all trade unions. Its limits in relation to trade unions do not appear to have been tested in any reported case; nor is it clear to what extent it has been affected by the prohibitions against actions in tort in section 4 of the 1906 Act. Most probably it has been extinguished.

3. ACTIONS BY OR AGAINST A REGISTERED UNION IN ITS OWN NAME

A registered union can sue or be sued in its registered name subject only to two exceptions:

1. Such actions are prohibited in respect of any tort committed by or on behalf of the union (section 4 of the Act of 1906).

2. This procedure cannot be used for the purpose of directly enforcing, or recovering damages for the breach of any of the contracts mentioned in section 4 of the 1871 Act, regardless of whether the trade union is lawful or unlawful at common law.

4. ACTIONS BY OR AGAINST THE TRUSTEES OF REGISTERED TRADE UNIONS UNDER SECTION 9 OF THE 1871 ACT

The Act of 1871 requires that all property of a registered trade union be held by and be under the control of the trustees of the union, and by section 9 of the Act the trustees are empowered to bring or defend any action, suit, prosecution, or complaint touching the property or any right or claim to property of the union.

This procedure is only available by or against the trustees of a registered union, and is subject to two exceptions:

1. It is not available in respect of any tort committed by or on behalf of a trade union in contemplation or furtherance of a trade dispute. Except in respect of trade disputes the procedure is expressly preserved in actions for tort by section 4 (2) of the 1906 Act.

2. It is not available for the purpose of directly enforcing or recovering damages for the breach of any of the contracts mentioned in section 4 of the 1871 Act, be the union lawful or unlawful at common law.

The section gives rise to a difficult question of construction which is this: are the legal proceedings contemplated limited to actions which concern specific property, or does any claim which threatens the general assets of the union fall within the scope of the section? In other words, is the section to receive a wide or a narrow construction? Within the narrow construction fall claims arising out of particular property, such as a breach of covenant in respect of land vested in the trustees. Within the wide construction would fall claims arising out of the general activities of the union, as for example a claim for damages for wrongful dismissal of an employee of the union, or libel published in the union's paper. The House of Lords have not yet resolved this question. In the meantime, the lower courts have in general accepted the wide construction. The secretary of a registered union, who was dismissed without proper notice, succeeded in an action against trustees under this section in recovering arrears of salary and damages for wrongful dismissal. Two actions for damages for libel contained in union publications were successful.

A distinction is therefore now drawn between a registered union and its trustees so as to render the property of such a union, in the hands of its trustees, liable for tortious acts committed on behalf of the union, otherwise than in contemplation or furtherance of a trade dispute.

5. ACTIONS BY OR AGAINST OFFICERS OF REGISTERED TRADE UNIONS AUTHORIZED BY THE RULES

Section 9 of the 1871 Act empowers registered unions to authorize one of their officers to sue or be sued in all proceedings which would lie against the trustees under the section. The authority must be given by the rules.

The same considerations apply to this procedure as apply to proceedings against the trustees, save for this: this procedure is not preserved by section 4 (2) of the 1906 Act, and as a result would not seem to be available to recover damages for any tort committed by or on behalf of a union.

Jurists frequently say that modern law, as opposed to archaic law, provides a remedy wherever there is a right which requires protection.

A glance at the restrictions imposed on actions against trade unions will show that this is not true of trade union law. Here the right depends on the availability of a remedy.

OFFICERS OF TRADE UNIONS

In some cases the only remedy of an aggrieved person may be against the officers of a union personally. This is so when an officer acts in excess of the powers given to him under the rules and sometimes when the right of action against the trade union is inhibited by statute.

The members of the committee of management of an unregistered union in entering into a contract on behalf of the union, become personally liable. In the absence of provision in the rules, they seem to have no right to be indemnified by the general body of members, although they may be entitled to contribution from other members of the committee.

In tort the members of the committee of management and other officers are protected by two provisions of the Acts: (1) section 1 of the 1906 Act provides that in a trade dispute a person shall not be liable in an action for conspiracy unless the offending act would be actionable without the element of conspiracy; (2) section 3 of the same Act provides that, in a trade dispute, the common-law tort of procuring a breach of contract of employment shall not be actionable.

CHAPTER XII

THE GENERAL STRIKE

THE most important and disturbing question arising out of modern trade-union legislation is whether a general strike is legal. No certain answer can be given. The problem became of immediate practical importance as soon as the sympathetic strike was made lawful by the Trade Disputes Act 1906.

No attempt was made to solve this problem in 1920, when a general strike threatened. To meet this threat Parliament passed the Emergency Powers Act of that year. Although this Act provides ample powers to fight a strike of large dimensions, it gives no power to stop one, and indeed specifically prohibits the making of regulations that would make it an offence to strike, or peacefully pursuade another to strike.

In 1926 came the General Strike. In the following year the 1927 Act was passed with the intention of preventing a repetition. This Act prohibited 'sympathetic strikes' and declared that strikes or lock-outs designed or calculated to coerce the Government, either directly, or indirectly by inflicting hardship on the community, were illegal.

The Socialist Party and the trade unions disliked this Act whole-heartedly, and in 1945 it was repealed. The result is that the answer to the question: 'Is a general strike legal?' has again become uncertain.

Lord Asquith, writing in 1927, said: 'A country whose law gives no clear answer to the question whether a general strike is legal or not, deserves a succession of general strikes to concentrate its mind.'

It is agreed on all hands that a strike with a political

object, as contrasted with an industrial one, cannot be de-
fended. A strike with the aim of putting pressure on the
Government so as to influence its foreign policy, or its policy
in regard to nationalization or de-nationalization of an industry is not within the protection of the Trade Union Acts.

Beyond this, opinion divides into two strongly opposed
schools of thought.

The answer seems to depend on two questions:

1. Is a strike of such magnitude that it brings pressure to
bear on the Government illegal at common law?

2. If so, is it, none the less, protected, if it is bona-fide action
taken in contemplation or furtherance of a trade dispute?

One school of thought contends that as strikes are not in
themselves illegal at common law, an act which is perfectly
lawful if done by a few cannot become unlawful merely because it is done by many.

The fact that the strike results in putting pressure on the
Government is, they say, immaterial, for every strike to a
lesser or greater degree may do so. The Ministry of Labour
constantly intervenes in trade disputes in order to avoid dis-
ruption of trade, and has strongly advocated restraint in
wage claims that are unrelated to increases in production.
If employers resist such demands on the ground of government policy, can it be said that strikes in favour of such
demands are illegal as being directed against the Government or nation? So to hold, would be to undermine the right
to strike itself. It would automatically prevent any strike in
the civil service or in a nationalized or essential industry.

Even if such a strike were unlawful at common law, it
would none the less be within the protection of the Trade
Union Acts, for a trade dispute has been so defined as to include a sympathetic strike. Therefore if the original dispute
has the particular industrial connexion required by the Act
of 1906, and, as the result of sympathetic action, it spreads to

other industries and becomes general, it remains within the protection of the Acts, however large it may grow.

The other school of thought base their argument upon the proposition that a strike that is calculated to coerce the Government is unlawful at common law, and is not within the protection of the Acts, because the Acts were never intended to apply to such a strike.

There can be little doubt that the Acts were not intended to apply to a strike calculated to coerce the Government. But there is some doubt as to whether such a strike is illegal at common law.

Much has been written upon the subject. The arguments on both sides have been stated and re-stated, and the uncertainty of the answer remains.

It may be that it will never be necessary to give a definite answer to the question. A review of the history of trade-union law suggests that uncertainty in the law has been a great deterrent. Since 1926 trade unions have come to show a responsible regard not only for the interests of their members but also for other sections of the community, and the community as a whole. As a result the necessity for a definite answer to the question has grown less pressing. Trade unionists have shown wisdom in refraining from testing the extreme limits of the privileges conferred on them.

Those who maintain that a general strike is unlawful, have some judicial authority in their favour (National Sailors' & Firemen's Union *v.* Reed (1926) Ch. 536). It is not an authority of great weight. The Judge who tried the case— Astbury J.—did not have the advantage of legal argument on both sides, as the defendants were not represented by Counsel, and much of what he said was not necessary to support his decision.

The case arose out of the General Strike of 1926, and the facts were as follows:

In order to avoid a reduction of coal-miners' wages, the

Government had granted a temporary subsidy which was due to end on the 30th April, 1926. A Royal Commission had been appointed to inquire into the economy of the industry, and its report recommending reorganization of the industry had been published.

Shortly before the 30th April, the mine-owners posted notices announcing that upon the termination of the subsidy the miners' wages would be reduced. The Miners Federation and the T.U.C. appealed to the Government to obtain the withdrawal of these notices. This having failed, they appealed to the Government to continue the subsidy. This also failed.

As the miners refused to accept the reduction in their wages, the industry came to a standstill. Thereupon the T.U.C. took steps to organize sympathetic strikes in essential industries and issued a manifesto stating that unless a settlement was reached which they could recommend to the miners, strikes in certain industries would follow.

No settlement was reached, and the strike followed. In some industries the strike was ordered by the union concerned, working in collaboration with the T.U.C. In other industries workers stopped work spontaneously, and without instructions.

The Sailors' and Firemen's Union instructed its members not to strike. The officers of one of its branches, in disregard of these instructions, called a strike. The union thereupon brought this action for an injunction to restrain the branch officials from calling a strike in contravention of the rules, and contrary to common law.

The action never reached trial. The union, however, applied for an interim injunction, which Astbury J. had no hesitation in granting. He held that the strike called by the branch officials was both unlawful at common law, unprotected by the Trade Union Acts, and in breach of the rules of the union.

CHAPTER XIII

CONCILIATION AND ARBITRATION

FOR some considerable time both sides in industry have in-
creasingly recognized that strikes and lock-outs are an ex-
pensive and damaging way of settling trade disputes, and,
with the assistance of the Government, the tendency now is
to try to settle such disputes by negotiation between the parties, and, if this fails, by arbitration.

This spirit animated the trade unions during the War
when they not only accepted but put into effect the Conditions of Employment and National Arbitration Order of
1940, which prohibited strikes and lock-outs until the dispute had been reported to the appropriate Minister and
twenty-one days had thereafter elapsed, provided that during that time the Minister did not refer the dispute to arbitration. This was the famous Order 1305, which has now
been replaced by the Industrial Disputes Order 1951 No.
1376. It repeals the provisions of the previous order prohibiting strikes and lock-outs, but it has preserved the provisions as to arbitration which are still effective, and which
we consider later in this Chapter.

Apart from this Order there are two Acts of Parliament
dealing with the subject: the Conciliation Act 1896, and the
Industrial Courts Act 1919.

As appears from its name, the first Act was intended to
facilitate conciliation in industrial disputes. The machinery
provided was the creation of what were known as Conciliation Boards constituted for the purpose of settling disputes between employers and workmen by conciliation or

arbitration. The Act gives the Board of Trade power to establish or encourage the establishment of such Boards in any district or trade in which no adequate means for conciliation existed.

The powers given to the Boards are:

(1) to inquire into the causes and circumstances of differences between workmen and employers, or different classes of workmen;

(2) to take steps to enable the parties to meet;

(3) to appoint a person to act as a conciliator or a board of conciliators, or, on the application of both sides, to appoint an arbitrator.

The powers of a conciliator under the Act are limited to inquiring into the causes and circumstances of the dispute, trying to bring about a settlement, and reporting to the Board of Trade.

There is a provision that if a settlement is reached, either by conciliation or arbitration, a memorandum of its terms is to be drawn up and a copy sent to the Board of Trade.

All the powers given to the Board of Trade under this Act have now been transferred to the Minister of Labour.

The Act was very useful in holding out the offer of government assistance and encouragement to parties to an industrial dispute who were prepared to be reasonable; but it is doubtful whether it now serves any useful purpose. Conciliation has become the normal method of approach, while the provisions of the Act facilitating arbitrations are out of date. First, they have been superseded by those contained in the Industrial Courts Act 1909 and the Industrial Disputes Order 1951; secondly, an arbitration can only take place under the 1896 Act if both parties agree, and thirdly, there are no provisions or machinery for enforcing an award, when made.

The Industrial Courts Act 1909, as appears from its title, was passed for the purpose of setting up an industrial court to deal with trade disputes. To quote the preamble: 'It is to provide for the establishment of an Industrial Court and Courts of Enquiry in connection with trade disputes and to make other provision for the settlement of such disputes.' The Act is divided into four parts. Part 1 deals with the Industrial Court, which is to be a standing court consisting of persons appointed by the Minister of Labour, of whom some are to be independent, some are to represent employers, some to represent workmen, and in addition there are to be one or more women.

The president of the court and the chairman of any division of the court is to be one of the independent persons selected by the Minister.

Section 2 provides that a trade dispute, whether existing or apprehended, may be reported to the Minister by either party, and the Minister shall thereupon take such steps as seem to him expedient for promoting a settlement. The steps he may take, if he thinks fit, and if both parties consent, are as follows:

(1) he may appoint one or more arbitrators to settle the dispute;
(2) he may refer it to the Industrial Court;
(3) he may refer it to a board of arbitrators consisting of persons nominated by both sides, with an independent chairman nominated by him.

He may also refer to the Industrial Court for advice, any matter relating to or arising out of a trade dispute.

He is prohibited from exercising these powers if under some agreement there are existing arrangements for settlement, by conciliation or arbitration, within the trade or industry concerned, unless both parties consent to his doing so,

H

or there has been a failure to reach a settlement by means of conciliation or arbitration.

This part of the Act carries the matter but little further. The Minister can only refer trade disputes to arbitration if both sides consent. He cannot apparently move at all unless one party reports the dispute to him, and in absence of agreement his powers are limited to taking the matter into consideration and taking such steps as seem to him expedient for settling it. An award of the Arbitration Court under this Act has precisely the same defect as an award under the Conciliation Act. It cannot be enforced.

The most useful part of the Act, and the one which has proved most beneficial, is the power given to the Minister to refer questions to the Industrial Court for report.

Part 2 of the Act, which deals with Courts of Inquiry, amplifies the powers of the Minister to go to the Industrial Court for advice. Where a trade dispute exists or is apprehended, and whether it has been reported to him or not, the Minister may inquire into the causes and circumstances of the dispute, and may refer any matters arising therefrom to a Court of Inquiry appointed by him, and the court may inquire into the matters so referred and report to the Minister. The appointment of this court is in the discretion of the Minister. He may make rules giving the court power to summon witnesses and call for documents, and power to take evidence on oath. This provision does not give the Minister any power to settle a dispute, but it enables him to obtain a comprehensive report for his own information and the information of the public. He can do this without the agreement of either party. These inquiries have frequently done much good by making public the facts of a dispute, its origin, and the conduct of the parties in relation to it.

Finally we must consider the complex provisions of the Industrial Disputes Order 1951.

Part 1 deals with reporting disputes to the Minister. Matters which can be reported are of two classes:

(1) disputes, and
(2) issues.

Disputes are further divided into two classes:

(1) where there is machinery for the voluntary settlement of terms and conditions of employment, and
(2) where there is no such machinery.

A dispute may be reported by:

(1) an organization of employers;
(2) an employer who is in dispute with his own workmen;
(3) a trade union.

The report must be in writing. The Minister can demand further particulars and can refuse to accept the report until he has full particulars. No person or organization is placed under any obligation to report a dispute.

The action the Minister may take when a dispute is reported to him is set out in Part 2, and depends on whether there is machinery for voluntary settlement. If there is, and if he thinks that machinery suitable for conciliation or arbitration, and if he also thinks that all practicable means of reaching a settlement through that machinery have not been exhausted, he refers the dispute to that machinery.

Where there is no such machinery, or where the dispute is referred to such machinery and there is failure to reach a settlement, he must refer the matter to the Industrial Disputes Tribunal created by the Order.

There are further limitations on the right to report a dispute. Where there is machinery for voluntary settlement, the person or body reporting the dispute must appear to the Minister to be a person or body who habitually takes part

in the settlement of terms and conditions of employment
through that machinery. Where there is no such machinery,
if the body reporting is a trade union or employers' organization it must appear to the Minister that such union or
organization represents a substantial proportion of the employers or workmen in the trade or industry, or section of
trade or industry, concerned.

It will be seen that the right to report is limited, and the
Order is not directed to encouraging any free right to report
disputes.

The term 'dispute' is defined as follows:

' "Dispute" does not include a dispute as to the employment or non-employment of any person or as to whether
any person should or should not be a member of any trade
union, but save as aforesaid, means any dispute between
an employer and workmen in the employment of that employer connected with the terms of the employment or
with the conditions of labour of any of those workmen.'

This would appear to exclude from the Order one of the
most prolific sources of dispute: a strike because the employer will not sack a man who is not a member of some particular union; i.e. an attempt by a union to establish a
'closed shop'.

The expression 'issue' means the question of whether a
particular employer should observe recognized terms and
conditions of employment.

The provisions concerning issues, in the Order, are as follows: Where: (1) in any trade or industry or any section of
a trade or industry in any district, terms and conditions of
employment are established which have been settled by
negotiation or arbitration by organizations of employers
and trade unions which represent substantial proportions of
the employers and workmen engaged in that trade or industry in that district; (2) an issue is reported to the Minister

as to whether an employer in that district should observe
such conditions; (3) the Minister is of opinion that the body
reporting the issue (whether an organization of employers or
a trade union) habitually takes part in the settlement of
terms and conditions of employment in the trade or industry
or section of the trade or industry concerned, the Minister
shall refer the 'issue' to the Industrial Disputes Tribunal.

Once the 'issue' is reported to the Tribunal that body
must decide:

(1) whether there are recognized terms and conditions
applicable to the case, and

(2) whether the employer concerned is observing them
or is observing terms and conditions not less
favourable.

If the answer to the first question is in the affirmative and
to the second in the negative, the Tribunal may order the
employer to observe the recognized terms and conditions or
other terms and conditions determined by the Tribunal to be
not less favourable than the recognized terms and conditions.

At first sight it may be difficult to see the difference between a 'dispute' and an 'issue'.

'Issue' means (1) a difference as to whether a particular
employer is observing local terms and conditions as settled
by the local negotiating machinery (whatever it may be) or
by arbitration, or gives his employees something as good or
better, and (2) if not, whether he should observe such terms
and conditions.

The distinction between a dispute and an issue is important, as was indicated in the case of R. *v.* Industrial Disputes Tribunal ex parte Technaloy Ltd. (1954 2 A.E. 75).
In that case an employer was not a party to, or observing,
the appropriate agreement, and the trade union concerned
reported the matter to the Minister as a dispute. The employers took the point that it was an 'issue', and applied to

the court for an order to prevent the Tribunal hearing the matter as a 'dispute'. The Divisional Court held that it was an 'issue' and not a 'dispute'.

The trade union appealed to the Court of Appeal. Two of the Lord Justices of Appeal held that the difference was a dispute, the other Lord Justice agreed with the Divisional Court that, if there was a difference, it was an 'issue', but he also held that on the facts of the case the Minister was entitled to refer the matter to the Tribunal as a 'dispute'.

It is to be noted that while a 'dispute' can be reported by a trade union, an employers' organization, or an employer, an 'issue' can only be reported by a trade union or an organization of employers.

Again if the matter is an 'issue', the employer can excuse himself for not observing the agreed terms and conditions of employment, if he can satisfy the Tribunal that he gives his employees equally favourable or better terms and conditions. There is no such specific provision in the case of 'disputes'.

Finally, as we have seen, there are various ways in which the Minister can deal with a dispute. His choice is much more restricted in the case of an 'issue'.

This order attempts to remedy the chief defect of the Acts of 1896 and 1919, by making the Orders of the Industrial Disputes Tribunal binding on the parties. Article 10 provides that where an award on an 'issue' or 'dispute' has been made by the Tribunal, as from the date of the award, or, as from some earlier date not being earlier than the date on which the 'issue' or 'dispute' first arose, it shall be an implied term of the contract between the employer and workers, to whom the award applies, that the terms and conditions of employment to be observed under the contract shall be in accordance with the award until varied by agreement or by a subsequent award of the Tribunal or until different terms are settled through the machinery of negotiation in the trade or industry.

Article 6 provides that where a dispute is settled by existing local machinery, any agreement decision or award shall 'for the purposes of this Order' be treated as constituting a final settlement of that dispute. Where a dispute has been settled by an award under the Conciliation Act or the Industrial Courts Act that award, again 'for the purposes of this Order', shall be treated as constituting a final settlement of that dispute.

It is difficult to see exactly what this means. As we have mentioned, a weakness of awards under these two Acts is that they are not binding. This Article says that they are 'to constitute a final settlement' for the purposes of the Order; but it does not follow that they are automatically to be read into the appropriate contracts of service.

The provision in Article 10 which enables the Tribunal to date back an award has already caused trouble and been the subject of proceedings in the High Court. It is difficult to identify the precise date on which an 'issue' or 'dispute' first arose.

Article 7 and the First Schedule provide the machinery for setting up the Tribunal. It consists of three appointed members, one of whom is to be chairman, and two other members, one representing employers, and the other the workers.

The Minister creates three panels, from whom the members of the Tribunal are appointed. One member is selected by him. The employers' representative is chosen by the Minister after consultation with the British Employers' Confederation. The workmen's representative is chosen by the Minister after consultation with the Trades Union Congress.

Unlike the Industrial Courts Act, women members are not made obligatory.

The quorum necessary to constitute a sitting is three: an appointed member in the Chair, and one each of the employers' and workmen's representatives.

The Minister appoints the Secretary of the Tribunal and such other officers and officials as he thinks necessary. The Tribunal regulates its procedure and proceedings as it thinks fit.

The Tribunal is not empowered to call for documents, enforce the attendance of witnesses, or administer oaths. It seems doubtful whether it can enforce the attendance of the parties if they choose to ignore its proceedings.

The Schedule contains an unusual but probably very useful provision in the following words:

'If any question arises as to the interpretation of any award of the Tribunal the Minister or any party to the award may apply for a decision on such question and the Tribunal shall decide the matter after hearing the parties, or without such hearing, provided the consent of the parties has been first obtained. The decision of the Tribunal shall be notified to the parties and shall have effect in the same manner as the decision in an original award.'

This would enable the Tribunal to clarify any ambiguity in its decisions. As the Tribunal must hear the parties, or obtain their consent to proceed in their absence, it would appear that a party can prevent such a hearing by not appearing, and by refusing to consent to the Tribunal proceeding in his absence.

Sub-paragraph (3) of Article 8 provides:

'Where it appears to the Minister in respect of a dispute reported to him . . . that action is being taken by either of the parties to the dispute designed to compel the acceptance of terms or conditions of employment which are the subject of the dispute and resulting in a stoppage of work or a substantial breach of an agreement between the parties, the Minister shall not refer that dispute to the Tribunal while such action continues if in his opinion it would be undesirable to do so and where the Minister has referred a dispute to the Tribunal and thereafter notifies the Tribunal that one of the parties is taking such action as aforesaid all proceedings thereon shall be stayed until the Minister cancels such notification.'

The effect of this provision is to give the Minister power to stop proceedings when either of the parties acts in an unreasonable manner.

While all parties in industry are conscious that 'direct action' is the worst possible way of settling disputes, and that the public at large have little sympathy for participants in strikes; neither side likes the existing machinery for arbitration. Both sides are suspicious of too much government interference. The workmen's trade unions in particular attach great value to the right to strike. They regard with suspicion anything they think is an attempt to curtail it. In the result, it is necessary to avoid any suggestion of compulsion in any proposals for conciliation or arbitration.

THE TRADE UNION ACTS, AND CERTAIN GENERAL ACTS AFFECTING TRADE UNIONS

* TRADE UNION ACT 1871. First of the modern Acts: contains protective provisions for trade unions, defines a trade union, provides for their registration and administration, restricts the enforcement of certain trade union contracts.

JUDICATURE ACT 1873. Resulted in enabling representative actions to be brought against trade unions in all Divisions of the High Court.

* CONSPIRACY & PROTECTION OF PROPERTY ACT 1875. Extends the statutory protections, imposes special penalties for the breach of certain contracts of service and for intimidation.

* TRADE UNION ACT AMENDMENT ACT 1876. Makes further administrative provisions for unions and amends the definition of a trade union.

PROVIDENT NOMINATIONS & SMALL INTESTACIES ACT 1883. Makes provisions affecting trade unions for the nomination and payment of death benefit.

FRIENDLY SOCIETIES ACT 1896. Places restrictions on the insurance of young children which apply to some trade unions.

CONCILIATION ACT 1896. Creates machinery for conciliation and arbitration by agreement in industrial disputes.

* TRADES DISPUTES ACT 1906. Extends the statutory protections, prohibits actions in tort against trade unions, authorizes peaceful picketing, defines trade dispute and workman.

ASSURANCE COMPANIES ACT 1909. Applies certain provisions relating to insurance to trade unions which are not registered or do not obtain exemption from the Board of Trade.

* TRADE UNION ACT 1913. Extends the definition of trade union, authorizes political objects and political fund, requires special rules for the political fund.

TRADE UNION (AMALGAMATION) ACT 1917. Provides for the amalgamation of trade unions.

INDUSTRIAL COURTS ACT 1919. Provides for the settlement of industrial disputes, establishes the Industrial Court, contains a new definition of industrial dispute and workman for purposes of the Act.

POLICE ACT 1919. Constitutes Police Federation, prohibits police officers from joining a trade union, makes it a criminal offence to cause disaffection in the police force.

ELECTRICITY ACT 1919. Extends the provisions of Act of 1875 relating to breaches of contracts of service to electricity undertakings.

EMERGENCY POWERS ACT 1920. Authorizes Parliament to make special regulations to meet an emergency, prohibits industrial conscription, and preserves the right to strike.

TRADE DISPUTE & TRADE UNION ACT 1927. This Act was passed after the General Strike of 1926, and is now repealed.

SOCIETIES (MISCELLANEOUS) PROVISIONS ACT 1940. Makes further provision for the amalgamation of trade unions.

TRADE DISPUTES & TRADE UNION ACT 1946. Repeals the Act of 1927.

ASSURANCE COMPANIES ACT 1946. Authorizes registered trade unions to carry on certain insurance business.

NATIONAL INSURANCE ACT 1946. Disqualifies contributors who are unemployed because of certain trade disputes from benefits under the Act.

NATIONAL ASSISTANCE ACT 1948. Makes like provisions in respect of public assistance grants.

COMPANIES ACT 1948. Preserves prohibition of incorporation of trade unions under the Act.

INDUSTRIAL ASSURANCE & FRIENDLY SOCIETIES ACT 1948. Prohibits insurance of young children by trade unions.

This is a formidable list, but in fact the only Acts which need consideration in detail are those marked with a star.

The remainder are either limited in application to a few unions, or to exceptional cases. We think it may be of use to the reader to have a full list of all the enactments at present in force which have provisions affecting trade unions or their members.

We have not included Statutory Orders.

The Act of 1927 has been wholly repealed by the Act of 1946.

INDEX

For Product Safety Concerns and Information please contact our EU
representative GPSR@taylorandfrancis.com
Taylor & Francis Verlag GmbH, Kaufingerstraße 24, 80331 München, Germany